C macdonald

WE WERE THERE

THE 20th CENTURY

WE WERE THERE

GODFREY CAWTE

Headmaster, Lord's Hill Primary School, Southampton

BASIL BLACKWELL OXFORD

Filmset and printed in the Republic of Ireland
by Hely Thom Ltd, Dublin

Bound by
Kemp Hall Bindery, Oxford

Contents

Acknowledgements

The author and publisher are grateful to the following for permission to reproduce copyright material:

John Murray for the extracts from *Scott's Last Voyage*.

Collins & Co Ltd for the extracts from *The Wooden Horse* by Eric Williams.

Allen & Unwin Ltd for the extracts from *The Kon-Tiki Expedition* by Thor Heyerdahl.

Putman & Co Ltd for the extracts from *The First Four Minutes* by Roger Bannister.

Geoffrey Bles Ltd for the extracts from *Phoenix at Coventry* by Sir Basil Spence.

Hodder & Stoughton Ltd for the extracts from *The Ascent of Everest* by Sir John Hunt.

Valentine Mitchell & Co for the extracts from *The Diary of Anne Frank*.

United States Information Service for the extracts from *A Walk in Space—Gemini 4—Extravehicular Activity*.

Weidenfeld & Nicolson Ltd for the extracts from *Laugh a Defiance* by Mary Richardson.

Paul Popper Ltd for the photographs on pages 3, 5 (top), 10, 11, 12, 14, 17.

Radio Times Hulton Picture Library for the photographs on pages 5 (bottom), 96, 98, 101, 103.

Sport and General Press Agency for the photographs on pages 43, 45, 46.

The Mount Everest Foundation for the photographs on pages 48, 49, 50, 52, 53, 55, 56, 57, 61.
United States Information Service for the photographs on pages 79, 81, 82, 84, 85, 86, 87, 88, 89.
Imperial War Museum for the photographs on pages 106, 107.
Camera Press for the photographs on pages 108, 109.

The author is particularly grateful to the following for their help in compiling this book: Arthur E. Lewis (for the Titanic interview), Herr Otto Frank, Sir Basil Spence, Canon Clifford E. Ross.

Titanic
the unsinkable liner

On April 10th, 1912 a great liner steamed out of Southampton Docks on her maiden voyage. She was the White Star liner, *Titanic*. Great crowds lined the dockside and stretched down the shores of Southampton Water to watch her departure. Ships sounded their sirens and the crowds cheered. This was a very special occasion. The liner was the largest vessel afloat. It was the most luxurious and it was expected to be the fastest and the safest. In fact, the owners claimed that the liner was unsinkable. All those on board— passengers, captain and crew—believed this too and so did all the people who had come to wave goodbye.

Four days later, when the ship was speeding through the North Atlantic on its way to New York, it struck an iceberg which ripped open the steel plates along the ship's side. Within three hours the *Titanic* had disappeared beneath the sea.

Nearly 1,500 passengers and members of the crew were drowned. Captain Smith, an experienced sailor, went down with his ship. Many of those on board were able to jump into the water—but died in the icy sea.

The following morning, a ship named the *Carpathia,* which had received wireless signals for help, arrived near the scene of the disaster and took 711 survivors on board. Among them was a young steward, MR. ARTHUR LEWIS. Unlike most of the men on board, he had been allowed into one of the lifeboats so that he could help with the rowing. 55 years later he described the sinking of the ship—and his rescue—to a group of children. Here are their questions and his actual answers taken from a tape-recording of his interview:

Q. What was the first you knew of the collision with the iceberg?

A. A steward, unknown to me, came into my cabin. He woke me up and said, 'If you want to see anyone else alive, you'd better get up because the ship is sinking.' He went out of the cabin and I saw him no more.

Q. You never discovered who he was?

A. I never knew who he was from that day to this—but he was the man who saved my life.

Q. When he said the ship was sinking, could you believe it?

A. No, when you get woken up and told a thing like that with sleepy eyes after a hard day's work, it makes you feel a bit queer.

Q. You weren't very old were you?

A. No, I was 22.

Q. You knew you had to get up—did you put on any special clothes?

A. No, I just put on odds and ends which I could find quickly.

Q. What was the story from that moment onwards?

A. I came out of the cabin and I got up into the working alleyway (where everybody walks) and I went right up into the bow of the ship. The water was coming over the gunwales of the ship (that's the edge of the deck, you know). I stood there for a moment and I said a prayer and after that I went up to the top decks.

When I got to the promenade deck, I saw three ladies, arm in arm, walking up and down. I said to the ladies, 'You'd better come along with me because the ship's sinking. We'll go up and see if there are any lifeboats we can get into.' So they said, 'We're all right, Steward, the ship CAN'T sink—so we'll stay where we are!' So off I went on my own to the boat deck.

There was only one boat left there in the corner. I started taking the canvas off the lifeboat. Then a sailor came along and helped me. We swung the boat out and an officer came up and he would only allow women and children into the boat. He asked me if I could row. I said, 'Yes'—so he said, 'Go into the boat and take the bow oar.'

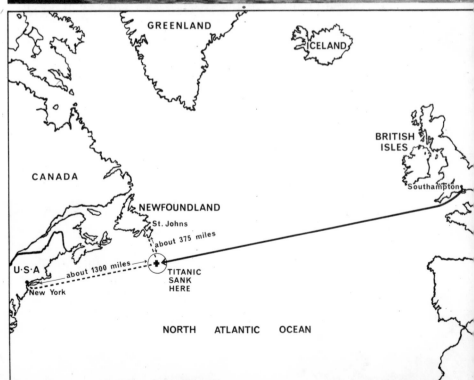

GREENLAND

ICELAND

BRITISH
ISLES

CANADA

NEWFOUNDLAND

St. Johns

about 375 miles

Southampton

U·S·A

about 1300 miles

New York

TITANIC
SANK
HERE

NORTH ATLANTIC OCEAN

We were full up with women and children. Their husbands weren't allowed in there so the wives just had to kiss their husbands goodbye. When the boat was completely filled up, we were lowered into the water. We untied the ropes each end and rowed away—and when I looked up at the ship, her bow was right under the water and the propellers were right up in the air.

When she was half way, there was a big crash—that was the engines which were on blocks. They went right through the bow of the ship—then she slid right down . . . and vanished. Then I heard the cries of the people who were drowning . . . and they didn't last very long. Then it was quiet—and it was very, very cold—but the water was calm.

Q. Were you able to pick up any of the people in the water?

A. No—they were too far away—and not only that, there wasn't room in the boat. It was weighed down right to the water's edge. If we had taken any more on, it would have turned the boat over and we would all have gone.

Q. Had you heard any guns fired by the crew?

A. No, but I did see red and green rockets going up in the air.

Q. Did you see the actual iceberg which sank the *Titanic*?

A. No. There were so many about that I didn't notice the actual one. But when I saw the water coming over the bow of the ship, there was ice as well where the ship had smashed the 'berg. It was like breaking a milk bottle.

Q. Had you radio on board the *Titanic*?

A. Yes, but it was not so powerful as it is now. They had to do all this tapping business.

Q. Did you know any of the other people in the boat with you?

A. No.

Q. What was it like in that boat all night?

A. Well, not too bad—but people were cold where they had no proper clothes. But I was rowing most of the time and that kept me warm. The people in the boat were very sad and miserable. They could hardly speak to each other and didn't know what to say or do.

Q. A ship called the *Californian* was nearby wasn't it?

A. It was supposed to be—but it has never been proved. There WAS a ship nearby. I saw the lights—but what ship it was no-one could say.

Q. What was the first you saw of the ship which rescued you?

A. We saw it in the distance and it came right up alongside of us. The people climbed out of the boat and on board of the *Carpathia*.

Q. Was your boat taken on board the *Carpathia*?

A. No. It was towed to America.

Q. When you were on board the *Carpathia,* you must have felt glad to have a good boat under you?

A. Yes! There was plenty of tea and coffee and things to eat. The passengers who had clothes fixed us up and when we arrived in New York, we went to a shed and there were a lot of people there with bags of clothes. I signed on another ship called the *Lapland* about a fortnight after that.

Q. You had to WORK your way back across the Atlantic?

A. Yes I did. I didn't want to think about the accident. We arrived at Plymouth where there was a special place for us to sleep—but we were not allowed outside of the Dock for a while.

Q. How long was it before you saw your wife after you returned to England?

A. Probably a month I expect—but I managed to send her a telegram from New York.

Q. How had she heard that you were safe?

A. My brother-in-law used to go down to the White Star Offices in Canute Road in Southampton where they put up the names of the saved on a board. One morning he saw my name (Lewis) up there and he said to his wife, 'What were his initials?' She said, 'A.E.R.' so he said, 'Well, he's safe!' They rushed home to tell my wife.

Q. How much did you earn for the whole voyage?

A. I had £3 15s.

Q. And nothing else was given to you afterwards?

A. No, not a halfpenny.

The disaster of the sinking of the *Titanic* was so sudden and so unexpected that, at first, the whole world seemed to be stunned with the shock.

Soon an enquiry into the reason for the disaster and for the loss of so many lives was held. As a result, future passengers and crews of ships were safeguarded in many ways. Small boats began to make ice-patrols in the North Atlantic Ocean so that large vessels could be warned of the danger if icebergs were floating about. Improvements were made in life-saving equipment and sufficient lifeboats were carried for everybody on board ships during their voyages, while 'Boat-Drill' was made compulsory on every voyage.

The wreck of the *Titanic* lies deep on the bed of the Atlantic Ocean. Within her hull are luxurious fittings, valuable cargo and hundreds of passengers and crew who went down with her.

Although the First World War broke out shortly afterwards, the sinking of the *Titanic* is still remembered as one of the most tragic disasters of all time. However, the laws of safety which were worked out after the disaster have protected the lives of countless sailors and passengers at sea from that night in April, 1912 . . . until today.

Scott of the Antarctic

Although failure is the opposite of success, sometimes, it is just as important as a success—and we can admire it just as much. Many people think that one of the most important 'failures' in history was the journey to the South Pole by Captain Robert Falcon Scott—the famous 'Scott of the Antarctic.'

Since he had been a boy, he had longed to be the first to do things. After he joined the Royal Navy he became a Captain and was able to become an explorer as well—to be the first person to see places which no one else had ever seen.

In 1906, there were not many unexplored parts of the world—but the part which fascinated Scott was that great cap of ice and snow covering its most southerly part: ANTARCTICA—with the South Pole at its centre. Little was known about this vast, icy desert and because conditions were so grim, few men had tried to discover its secrets.

Accompanied by another great explorer, Ernest Shackleton, Scott had led an expedition to the Antarctic in 1902. (The ship they used, the *Discovery,* may be seen anchored near Waterloo Bridge on the River Thames in London.) Scott did not try to reach the South Pole on this occasion—but he did learn a great deal about staying alive in that part of the world.

Captain Scott was anxious to explore the south further and hoped as well that he, an Englishman might be the first man to reach the South Pole and perhaps fly the Union Jack on that spot before the flag of any other nation flew there.

Many men with the love of adventure in their hearts were anxious to go with this handsome and daring young explorer.

8

Finding members of the party was not difficult—but finding enough money for the expedition seemed almost impossible. Scott travelled many miles giving talks about the Antarctic and persuading the public to give money so that British explorers could pioneer the way to the Pole.

By 1910, all was ready for the expedition to set out on board its own ship—the *Terra Nova*.

Meanwhile, Captain Scott had married. His son, Peter, was too young to know his father because Scott left for the Antarctic about a year after his birth.

One of the objects of the expedition was to carry out a great deal of research and much information was recorded about this part of the world. One member of the party was an outstanding photographer, H. G. Ponting, who, with his early photographic equipment, took many memorable photographs. Overleaf are two of his photographs showing the *Terra Nova* frozen into the ice pack soon after its arrival.

11

Only a few of the men could be allowed to make the final journey to the Pole and it was very difficult for Scott to decide which members of the party should go. Every single man wished to accompany him. After much thought he selected these:

Captain Lawrence E. G. Oates; Petty Officer Edgar Evans; Lieutenant Henry Bowers; Dr. Edward Wilson.

Scott had planned three ways of making their journey easier. He hoped to use motor sledges, tough ponies and husky dogs. This was a good idea—but soon it was proved that the low temperatures and the difficult conditions would prevent him, and his four companions, from using anything of the kind for the journey. They would have to rely on their own feet.

At last they were ready to set off on the final stage of their journey to the Pole itself. They left bases all along the way in which food and fuel were stored for their use on the return journey.

Scott and his friends did reach the Pole—but they were not the first. While they were actually struggling towards their goal, over the Great Ice Barrier, through fierce blizzards and across miles of snow, a Norwegian, Roald Amundsen, had reached it about a month previously. The Norwegian flag was already flying there!

Throughout his journey, Scott kept a careful record of everything which happened to the expedition. Although writing was difficult for him, he wrote down his thoughts at that time. His journal contains a vivid account of their excitement as they neared the Pole, their uneasy feeling that they would be beaten to it—and the bitter disappointment of the five men before they began their long return journey.

1912.

Night, January 15th. Temperature Minus 25°. We made a capital afternoon march of 6·3 miles bringing the total for the day to over 12 miles. It is wonderful to think that two long marches would land us at the Pole. We left our depot today with nine day's provisions, so that it ought to be a certain thing now, and only the apalling possibility the sight of the Norwegian flag forestalling ours. Only 27 miles from the Pole. We *ought* to do it now.

Tuesday, January 16th. Temperature Minus 23·5°. The worst has happened, or nearly the worst. We marched well in the morning and covered 7½ miles. We started off in high spirits in the afternoon, feeling that tomorrow would see us at our destination. Bowers' sharp eyes detected a black speck ahead. Soon we knew that this could not be a natural snow feature. We marched on, found that it was a black flag tied to a sledge bearer; near by the remains of a camp; sledge tracks and ski tracks going and coming and the clear traces of dogs' paws—many dogs. This told us the whole story. The Norwegians have forestalled us and are first at the Pole. It is a terrible disappointment, and I am very sorry for my loyal companions. Tomorrow we must march on to the Pole and then hasten home with all the speed we can compass. All the day-dreams must go; it will be a wearisome return.

Wednesday, January 17th. Temperature Minus 22°. The Pole. Yes, but under very different circumstances from those expected. We have had a horrible day. Great God! this is an awful place and terrible enough for us to have laboured to it without reward of priority. Well, it is something to have got here. Now for the run home and a desperate struggle. I wonder if we can do it.

13

The following day (Thursday, January 18th, 1912) the explorers reached the tent which had been left behind by Amundsen. Inside they found some gifts and a letter to Scott written by Amundsen himself.

Scott's Diary takes up the story:

Left a note to say I had visited the tent with companions. We built a cairn, put up our poor slighted Union Jack, and photographed ourselves—mighty cold work all of it. Well, we have turned our back now on the goal of our ambition and must face our 800 miles of solid dragging—and good-bye to most of the day-dreams!

This is a copy of the photograph which they took at the South Pole. It is one of the most remarkable photographs ever taken. The negative was not developed for months and not one of the men in the picture ever saw it. You can see the Union Jack in the background. The photograph was taken by Lieutenant Bowers (sitting down on the left). He pulled a string attached to the shutter of the camera so that all five men could be in the photograph—he had to remove his glove to do so. Their leader, Captain Scott is in the middle of the back row.

Two of the five died before they reached their last camp. P. O. Evans had died in the middle of February from the effects of frostbite and the rigours of the journey. After a further month of endurance another of the survivors showed signs of great distress. This was Captain Titus Oates. He was suffering from frostbite in both feet which caused intense pain when trudging through the snow and ice. Oates soon realised that his own slow progress was becoming a tremendous handicap to his three friends who were wasting precious hours because he was slowing them down. Few men would have had the courage to suggest (as he did) that his companions should go on without him and leave him to a lonely and a certain death.

Friday, March 16th or Saturday, 17th. Lost all track of dates, but think the last correct. Tragedy all along the line. At lunch, the day before yesterday, poor Titus Oates said he couldn't go on. He proposed we should leave him in his sleeping bag. That we could not do, and we induced him to come on, on the afternoon march. In spite of its awful nature for him he struggled on and we made a few miles. At night he was worse and we knew the end had come.

Should this be found I want these facts recorded. Oates' last thoughts were of his mother. We can testify to his bravery. He has borne intense suffering for weeks without complaint, and to the very last was able and willing to discuss outside subjects. He did not—and would not—give up hope till the very end. He was a brave soul. This was the end. He slept through the night before last, hoping not to wake; but he woke in the morning—yesterday. It was blowing a blizzard. He said, 'I am just going outside and may be some time.' He went out into the blizzard and we have not seen him since.

We knew that poor Oates was walking to his death, but though we tried to dissuade him, we knew it was the act of a brave man and an English gentleman. We all hope to meet the end with a similar spirit, and assuredly the end is not far.

The death of Captain Oates was a tragic yet heroic incident and it stands out among the great number which occurred during the march. For a hero, like Captain Scott, to have written about him with such admiration was the greatest tribute which Oates could have wished for himself. Yet Scott's words in his diary for this day show that, by now, he and his companions had realized that the end was near.

The three who were left pitched their tent for the last time towards the end of March. Scott went on writing in his diary until just before he died and this is what he wrote as his very last entry:

> Every day we have been ready to start for our depot *11 miles* away, but outside the door of the tent it remains a scene of whirling drift. I do not think we can hope for better things now. ✳ We shall stick it out to the end, but we are getting weaker of course and the end cannot be far. It seems a pity, but I do not think I can write more—
>
> R. Scott
>
> Last entry For God's sake look after our people

None of us can imagine the effort which this must have been for him just before his death. Opposite there is a copy of the last entry. The actual page can be seen in the British Museum in London.

Apart from this last message, he managed—somehow—to write to a number of his friends, to the wives of his companions and to his own wife. He thought of his son, of course, and asked his wife to

> Make the boy interested in natural history if you can. It is better than games. They encourage it in some schools. I know you will keep him in the open air. What lots and lots I could tell you of this journey. What tales you would have for the boy.

One of the saddest things about Scott's death was that he did not live to see his son grow up. Peter Scott did become interested in natural history. In fact he probably knows more about birds and wild-life than anybody in the country. He is famous for his paintings of birds—and, more important, he has, through his television appearances made thousands of adults and children interested in the subject too!

Although the rest of the expedition (waiting back at their main base) realized that the five men must have died, they could not set out to find them until much later. Surgeon E. L. Atkinson, one of the men who found Scott's last camp, described what they found on November 12th, 1912.

Eight months afterwards we found the tent. It was an object partially snowed up and looking like a cairn. Inside the tent were the bodies of Captain Scott, Doctor Wilson and Lieutenant Bowers. Wilson and Bowers were found in the attitude of sleep, their sleeping bags closed over their heads as they would naturally close them.

Scott died later. He had thrown back the flaps of his sleeping bag and opened his coat. The little wallet containing the three

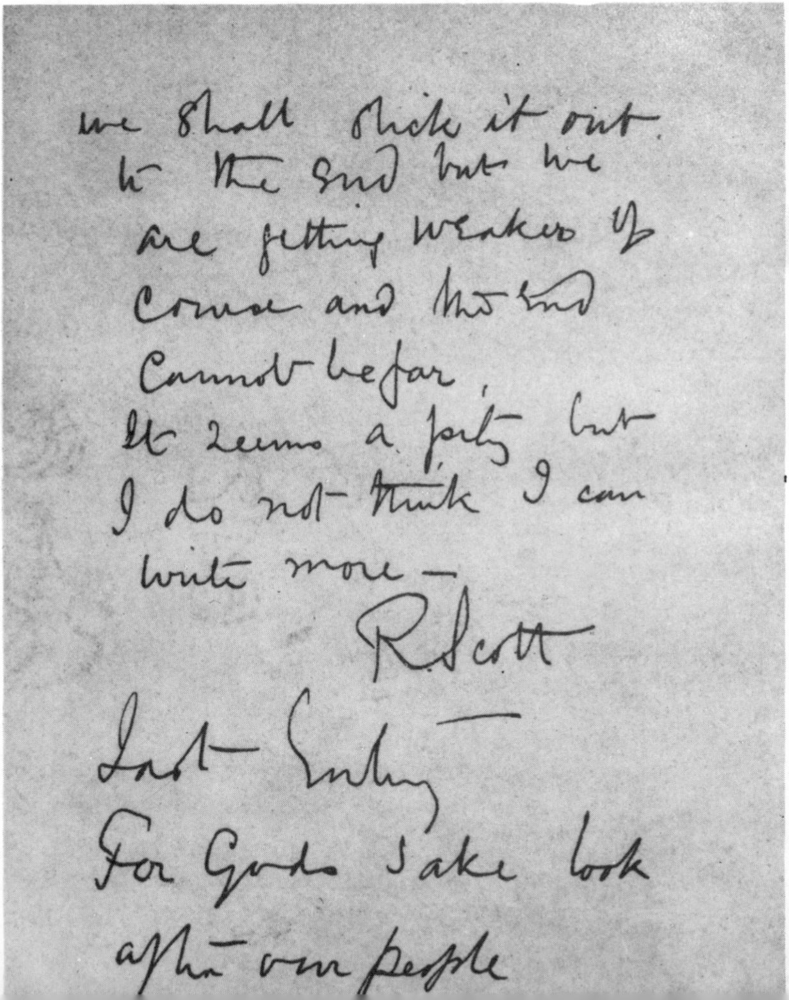

we shall stick it out
to the end but we
are getting weaker of
course and the end
cannot be far,
It seems a pity, but
I do not think I can
write more —

R Scott

Last Entry —
For Gods sake look
after our people

notebooks was under his shoulders, and his arm flung across Wilson. From Captain Scott's diary I found the reasons for this disaster.

When everything had been gathered up, we covered them with the outer tent and read the Burial Service. From this time until well into the next day we started to build a mighty cairn above them. This cairn was finished the next morning, and upon it a rough cross was placed, made from the greater portion of two skis.

Before the expedition finally left the Antarctic in the following January, a large cross was placed at the top of a hill overlooking the entire Antarctic. Under the names of the five men who had died, were written these lines from a poem by Lord Tennyson:

To strive, to seek,
To find,
And not to
Yield.

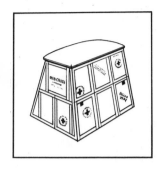

The Wooden Horse

During the Second World War (1939–1945) there were so many prisoners that special Prison Camps were set up. In Germany, many of the British prisoners were the pilots and crews of the bombers shot down during air raids on Europe.

The Germans built many of their camps in the middle of deep forests. The buildings where the 'P.O.W's' lived were only wooden huts—but it was just as difficult for the prisoners to escape from the camp itself as if they had been put in a real prison. First, there was a large space between the huts and the edge of the clearing. Next . . .

Fifteen feet inside the main fence was a single strand of barbed wire, twelve inches above the ground. This was a trip wire and anyone stepping over it was shot by the guards.

Beyond this was the main fence . . .

The wire itself, the main feature of the camp, was strong and heavily interlaced—a twelve foot double fence of bristling spikes. There were arc lamps hanging above the wire and along each fence stood small sentry boxes on stilts higher than the wire. These were armed with machine guns and carried searchlights which swept the camp continually during the hours of darkness. Guards carrying Tommy Guns patrolled the wire between the Sentry Boxes.

The Prisoners-of-War with nothing to do soon became bored. Their thoughts were of escape, of reaching the coast, of finding a boat, of seeing their families and friends—and of joining in the war again.

There was really only one way to escape—to dig a tunnel starting inside one of the huts, leading UNDERNEATH the wire and coming to the surface OUTSIDE the circle of barbed wire—giving the prisoners a chance to escape through the forest in the darkness.

Each attempt was carefully planned. ERIC WILLIAMS, an English airman, was imprisoned in 'Stalag Luft III', a German P.O.W. Camp. After the war he wrote a book telling the story of one of the most ingenious and famous escapes ever made. Since the escape depended upon the help of so many men, he wrote his book as if he, himself, had not been concerned. In the book he calls himself by another name—'Peter.' He saw one attempt to build a tunnel end in failure. He, and two of his friends, were talking about the unsuccessful attempt one day . . .

'Pity about Bill's scheme,' Peter said. 'I thought they stood a good chance with that.'

'It was too far from the wire,' John told him. 'Think of all the sand you've got to hide to dig a tunnel three hundred feet long. The only way to get out is to make the tunnel as short as possible —start somewhere out here, near the trip-wire.'

'You couldn't do it. There's nowhere near the wire to start a tunnel from. They chose the nearest building to the wire.'

'Why start from a building at all?' Why not start out in the open here—camouflage the trap. We could come out to it every day and take it slowly.'

'But that's impossible. It's like the top of a billiard table. Every spot of ground near the trip wire is in full view of at least three sentry boxes. Besides, how would you get the sand away?'

The men went on thinking. A few days later they were talking again—about escape, of course! Eric Williams remembered their conversation. One of the prisoners said:

'What about the Wooden Horse of Troy?' Peter laughed. 'The Wooden Horse of Troy?'

[He was thinking of an enormous wooden horse, built by the Greeks in 1180 B.C. They had been trying to capture the city of Troy for many months, but the Trojans had defended it so well that it was impossible to enter the city by using force.

The horse was wheeled to a position just outside of the city and left. The Greek army PRETENDED to go away—as if they had given up their attempt to capture the city. They knew (but the Trojans did not) that inside the great wooden horse a few brave and clever soldiers were hidden.

That night, the Trojans were so curious that they opened the gates of the city and wheeled the horse into the main square. They did not guess that there was anything inside it. When they had gone to their homes and all was quiet, the Greek soldiers climbed out through a trap door, opened the gates and the entire army, which had returned secretly in the dark, entered and captured the city quite easily.]

'Yes, but a vaulting horse, a box horse like we had at school. You know, one of those square things with a padded top and sides that go right down to the ground. We could carry it out every day and vault over it. One of us would be inside digging while the others vaulted. We'd have a good strong trap and sink it at least a foot below the surface. It's foolproof.'

'What about the sand?'

'We'll have to take it back with us in the horse. Use a kitbag or something. We'll have to keep the horse in one of the huts and get the chaps to carry it out with one of us inside it. We'll take the sand back with us when we go in.'

'It'll have to be strong.'

'Oh, we'll manage it all right.'

John could see it as a complete thing. The wooden vaulting horse, the vertical shaft under it and the long straight tunnel. He could see them working day after day until they got the tunnel dug. And he saw them going out through the tunnel.

'Let's go and see the Escape Committee now,' he said.

'There's no hurry. Let's get the whole thing worked out first.'

'We'll go NOW,' John said. 'Someone else might think of it while we're still talking about it.'

The 'Escape Committee' was a group of senior officers who

listened to prisoners' ideas for escaping. They made sure that not too many were trying to escape at once, they made arrangements for other prisoners to help if they were needed and they were able to provide money and clothes for use outside the camp when an escape had been successful. Quite often they would not agree to a plan if they thought it would fail. No prisoner would continue with a plan if the Escape Committee did not agree to help them. After listening to Eric Williams and his friends, they agreed to let them try—and they promised to help them in every possible way.

Digging the tunnel was a slow job. For a while, the prisoners did not even try to start digging. They wanted to make the guards familiar with the sight of prisoners vaulting over a horse—and enjoying it!

However, this was not enough. They had to ensure that the Germans saw INSIDE the box. To invite them to look might have aroused their suspicions. An 'accident' was arranged with great care! One of the vaulters pretended to be very awkward. The other prisoners pretended to laugh at his lack of skill . . . and the guards were delighted to join in the general laughter.

The standard of vaulting was high. The captain of the team led his men in a complicated series of jumps. Only one of the men was not so good. His approach was clumsy and his vaulting not up to the standard of the others. The guards soon singled him out as the butt of the party and grinned whenever he failed to clear the horse. The vaulting had drawn a crowd of amused prisoners, who jeered and cat-called whenever he made his run up to the box. Every time he failed to clear the horse he drew a guffaw of laughter from the surrounding prisoners.

Soon the guards in the boxes were leaning on their elbows waiting for him to make his run. It was not often they had the chance to laugh at the British prisoners. The boot was usually on the other foot. The more the spectators laughed the more determined this man appeared to be to clear the obstacle. He took a final, desperate leap and in missing his footing he lurched into the horse and knocked it over. He knocked it over on to its side so that the interior was in full view of the guards.

The horse was empty. The vaulters righted the box and went on with their sport. Soon they carried their horse back into the canteen, where they left it until the following afternoon.

Before they left the canteen they tied pieces of black cotton across the doorway and from the edge of the horse to the skirting board. The following morning the cotton was broken. The ferrets were taking no chances. During the night the vaulting-horse had been examined.

Once they knew the horse was harmless and that it was being used only for vaulting, the Germans stopped taking very much notice of it. The digging began.

The sand which was dug out of the tunnel was carried back to the horse in small sacks and hung on hooks inside. The digger would crawl back along the tunnel, out of the trap door and back into the inside of the horse. He covered the entrance to the tunnel with boards and on top of these he scattered loose sand so that the entrance would be invisible when the horse (with the prisoner inside it) was removed.

Of course, they met many difficulties and their tunnel was nearly discovered on many occasions. Once, when it had reached half way towards the outside, it fell in and one of the vaulters had to pretend that he was hurt. A stretcher was brought and, as he was being lifted on to it, the hole in the sand was covered up.

Eric Williams (he is 'Peter'), went down the next afternoon.

Peter found the tunnel choked with sand. Soft shifting sand that continued to fall as he worked. He worked in the dark, entirely by feel, and the air was bad so that he panted as he worked. Sand fell into his eyes and his mouth. He worked furiously clearing the sand away and fitting the shoring into position.

When he finally got back into the horse he could hardly find the strength to replace the trap. He put it back, and the sand above it, and gave John the signal that he was ready to be taken in. When he reached the canteen he crawled from the horse and fainted.

That evening he was taken to the camp hospital. It was a total collapse. He had taken too much out of himself with the digging, the vaulting and the worry. The British doctor prescribed a week in bed. The matter was out of Peter's hands and he lay in bed wondering what John was doing.

During the week he was in hospital no digging was done; but the horse was taken out every afternoon to avoid the suspicion of the guards.

After working all through the summer and well into the winter, the tunnel extended across the clearing, underneath the barbed wire and ended just below the surface OUTSIDE the wire.

Three men were to make an attempt to escape through the tunnel. They could not all go out in the box in one journey because someone had to remain in the box and scatter sand over the entrance so that it would be invisible to the guards. Usually only two men were carried inside.

'Peter' and John were taken out first but they carried the luggage which was needed for the escape as well. John (with the luggage) was left inside the tunnel while 'Peter' disguised the entrance and was taken back to the huts inside the horse.

The next—and last—journey with the horse was the most difficult. THREE men had to go—the two remaining escapers and one extra man who would seal off the entrance. The lightest man in the camp was chosen to do this because the prisoners carrying the box could have lifted no more weight. In addition, the vaulting horse itself was beginning to show signs of wear and could have fallen apart at any moment!

The two men climbed into the tunnel and, after sealing off the entrance, the third man was taken back to the safety of the huts.

It was an anxious time for the three men left inside the tunnel. They had to wait until it was dark before they could dig up to the surface and escape . . .

'We'd better push up to the top now,' Peter whispered. 'We've got to be out in half an hour.'

John nodded his agreement and began to push the tunnel up towards the surface. It was farther than they had expected and they thought they would never get to the top. Finally John broke through—a hole as large as his fist—and through it he caught his first glimpse of the stars. The stars in the free heavens beyond the wire.

'I'll break out the whole width of the tunnel,' John whispered, 'just leaving the thin crust over the top. Then we can break that quickly and there'll be less chance of being seen.'

At exactly six o'clock they broke through to the open air.

Peter stuck his head out of the tunnel and looked towards the camp. It was brilliantly floodlit. He had not realised how brilliantly it was lit. But the raised sentry boxes were in darkness and he could not see whether the guards were looking in his direction or not. He lifted out his kitbag and pushed it towards the ditch, wriggling himself out of the hole and rolling full length on the ground towards the ditch. He expected every minute to hear the crack of a rifle and feel the tearing impact of its bullet in his flesh.

He picked up his kitbag and ran blindly towards the pine forest on the other side of the road where John was waiting for him.

The adventures of the three airmen were not over when they managed to escape from the camp itself. In fact, the second part of their escape was as exciting as the first. They still had to find a boat to England. To do this they had to make a long journey through European countries occupied by the Germans—who were constantly on the look-out for escaped Prisoners-of-War.

At last, the three met again in Sweden. They had travelled separately because they thought it would be safer. They enjoyed sleeping in comfortable beds, eating good food and, most of all, they looked forward to returning to England and joining in the war again—against their former captors.

This they did and each man played his part again in the fight to win the Second World War.

By escaping in the way they did, they earned themselves a small place in history—though not as important a place as those who had used the first Wooden Horse over 3,000 years before.

Kon-Tiki

If you have ever held a piece of balsa wood in your hand, you will know that it is very light and very soft. It is ideal for making models (especially model aeroplanes) because it is so easy to cut and to shape.

A Norwegian called Thor Heyerdahl once had an idea—and balsa wood played a very important part in it. He wanted to risk his life sailing a raft made of balsa wood across the stormy seas of the Pacific Ocean. He wanted to prove that the idea which had come to him would work, and, as important ideas often do, this one occurred to him quite suddenly—although it must have been in the very back of his mind for a long time.

Before the Second World War, Thor Heyerdahl and his wife lived on Fatuhiva, a tiny island in the vast Pacific Ocean, for nearly a year. Tremendous distances separated the island (and hundreds of other small islands like it) from any of the great continents.

They were collecting plants and stones and objects as part of a study they were making of ancient civilizations. He remembers the evening when, by accident, his wife had said something which brought the idea to the forefront of his mind.

On that particular evening we sat as so often before, down on the beach in the moonlight, with the sea in front of us. Wide awake and filled with the romance that surrounded us, we let no impression escape us. We filled our nostrils with an aroma of rank jungle and salt sea, and heard the wind's rustle in leaves and palm tops. At regular intervals all other noises were drowned by the great breakers that rolled straight in from the sea and rushed in

27

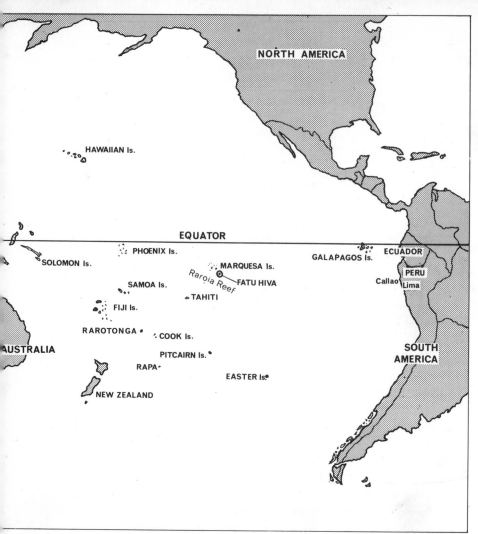

foaming over the land till they were broken up into circles of froth among the shore boulders. There was a roaring and rustling and rumbling among millions of glistening stones, till all grew quiet again when the sea-water had withdrawn to gather strength for a new attack on the invincible coast.

'It's queer,' said my wife, 'but there are never breakers like this on the other side of the island.'

'No,' said I, 'but this is the windward side, there's always a sea running on this side.'

28

We went on sitting there and admiring the sea which, it seemed, never wanted to give up demonstrating that here it came, rolling in from eastward, eastward, eastward. It was the eternal east wind, the trade wind, which had disturbed the sea's surface, dug it up and rolled it forward, up over the horizon to the east and over here to the islands. Here the unbroken advance of the sea was finally shattered against cliffs and reefs, while the east wind simply rose above coast and woods and mountains and continued westward unhindered, from island to island, towards the sunset.

So had the seas and the light cloud formations rolled up over the same eastern horizon since the morning of time. The first men who reached these islands knew well enough that this was so. And we knew ourselves that far, far below the horizon to eastward, where the clouds came up, lay the open coast of South America. It was 4,300 sea miles away, and there was nothing but sea between.

Sitting with them was an old, old man, a native of the island. He was poking a small fire with a stick.

'Tiki,' the old man said quietly, 'he was both god and chief. It was Tiki who brought my ancestors to these islands where we live now. Before that we lived in a big country beyond the sea.' . . . How old he was we did not know, but his wrinkled, bark-brown, leathery skin looked as if it had been dried in the sun and wind for a hundred years. He was certainly one of the few on these islands who still remembered and believed his father's and grandfather's legendary stories of the great Polynesian chief-god Tiki, son of the sun.

This was the beginning of the idea. Just before Heyerdahl went to sleep that night in his tiny hut near the sea, he said to his wife,

'Have you noticed that the huge stone figures of Tiki up in the jungle are remarkably like the gigantic monoliths which are relics of extinct civilisations in South America?'
I felt sure that a roar of agreement came from the breakers. And then they slowly subsided, while I slept.

29

He had remembered the great carved stones which he had seen in South America. Had men, somehow, crossed the thousands of miles of ocean—thousands of years ago?

The idea was born, but Heyerdahl had to wait patiently for several years. The Second World War broke out. He returned to Norway to fight for his country—but he went on thinking about Tiki . . . Kon-Tiki . . . Sun-Tiki . . . *Son of the Sun.*

When the war had ended, he went to a museum in New York to find out as much as he could about the Pacific Islands and also about the people who had lived in South America ruled by Kon-Tiki. He spoke to a historian who worked in the museum and mentioned his idea to him. The historian thought for a while but could not encourage Thor Heyerdahl.

'One thing we do know for certain—that none of the peoples of South America got over to the islands in the Pacific.'

He looked at me searchingly, and continued:

'Do you know why? The answer's simple enough. They couldn't get there. They had no boats.'

'They had rafts,' I objected hesitatingly. 'You know, balsa-wood rafts.'

The old man smiled and said quietly:

'Well, you can always TRY a trip from Peru to the Pacific Islands on a balsa-wood raft.'

Still, Heyerdahl refused to forget his idea. He talked to his friends and soon five young men agreed to help him prove that he was right—but they knew, and Heyerdahl knew that they were all risking their lives.

They spent many hours talking about their voyage—about winds and currents, about waves and weather, about the raft itself and how to control it. First they had to find balsa trees of the right size.

The old Peruvian rafts were built of balsa wood, which in a dry state is lighter than cork. The balsa tree grows in Peru, but only beyond the mountains in the Andes range, so the seafarers in Inca times went up along the coast to Ecuador, where they felled their huge balsa trees right down on the edge of the Pacific. We meant to do the same.

[They went to the forests of Ecuador and began their search.]

We soon found our way to an open place where there was a gigantic old tree. It towered high above the trees round about, and the trunk was three feet thick.

We swung the axe and drove it into the balsa trunk till the forest echoed our blows. But cutting a sappy balsa was like cutting cork with a blunt axe; it simply rebounded, and I had not delivered many strokes of the axe before Herman had to relieve me. The axe changed hands time after time, while the splinters flew and the sweat trickled in the heat of the jungle.

Later in the day Ku (the name given to the tree) was standing like a cock on one leg, quivering under our blows; soon he tottered and crashed down heavily over the surrounding forest, big branches and small trees being pulled down by the giant's fall.

31

When enough of the gigantic trees had been felled, they were floated down a nearby river and taken by boat to Callao Bay in Peru. This was where Heyerdahl thought the original rafts had started their long voyages.

It was time to put the raft together. Only materials actually available when the original rafts were being constructed were allowed. This bold decision probably saved their lives.

Nine of the thickest logs were chosen as sufficient to form the actual raft. Deep grooves were cut in the wood to prevent the ropes which were to fasten them and the whole raft together from slipping. Not a single spike, nail or wire rope was used in the whole construction. The nine great logs were first laid loose side by side in the water so that they might all fall freely into their natural floating position before they were lashed securely together. The longest log, 45 feet long, was laid in the middle and projected a long way at both ends. Shorter and shorter logs were laid symmetrically on both sides of this, so that the sides of the raft were 30 feet long, and the bow stuck out like a blunt plough.

When the nine balsa logs were lashed securely together with separate lengths of inch and quarter inch hemp rope, the thin balsa logs were made fast crossways over them at intervals of about three feet. The raft itself was now complete, laboriously fastened together with about three hundred different lengths of rope, each firmly knotted. A deck of split bamboos was laid upon it, fastened to it in the form of separate strips, and covered with loose mats of plaited bamboo reeds. In the middle of the raft, but nearer the stern, we erected a small open cabin of bamboo canes, with walls of plaited bamboo reeds and a roof of bamboo slats with leathery banana leaves overlapping one another like tiles. Forward of the cabin we set up two masts side by side. They were cut from mangrove wood as hard as iron, and leaned towards one another, so that they were lashed together crosswise at the top. The big rectangular square-sail was hauled up on a yard made of two bamboo stems bound together to secure double strength.

The whole construction was a faithful copy of the old vessels in Peru and Ecuador except for low splashboards in the bows, which later proved to be entirely unnecessary.

When the raft had been completed to Thor Hayerdahl's satisfaction, it was ready for the launching ceremony. The time had come to give the raft a name.

Gerd Vold, the expedition's secretary and contact on the mainland, was to christen the raft with milk from a coconut, partly to be in harmony with the Stone Age, and partly because, owing to a misunderstanding, the champagne had been put at the bottom of Torstein's private box. When our friends had been told in English and Spanish that the raft was named after the Incas' great forerunner—the sun-king who had vanished westward over the sea from Peru and appeared in Polynesia 1500 years ago— Gerd Vold christened the raft *Kon-Tiki*. She smashed the coconut (cracked) so hard against the stem that milk and seeds filled the hair of all those who stood reverently around.

Then the bamboo yard was hauled up and the sail shaken out, with Kon-Tiki's bearded head, painted in red by the artist Erik, in its centre. It was a faithful copy of the sun-king's head cut in red stone on a statue in the ruined city of Tiahuanaco.

33

At last they set out. At first, they found difficulties—mainly because they were trying to do too much themselves. The raft obeyed the winds and the currents flowing westward. Even during heavy storms, the Kon-Tiki raft looked after itself!

When swallowed up by the darkness, we heard the general noise from the sea around us suddenly deafened by the hiss of a roller close by, and saw a white crest come groping towards us on a level with the cabin roof, we held on tight and waited uneasily to feel the masses of water smash down over us and the raft. But every time there was the same surprise and relief. The 'Kon-Tiki' calmly swung up her stern and rose skyward unperturbed, while the masses of water rolled along her sides.

The ropes took the whole pressure. All night we could hear them creaking and groaning, chafing and squeaking. It was like one single complaining chorus round us in the dark, each rope having its own note according to its thickness and tautness. Every morning we made a thorough inspection of the ropes. We were even let down with our heads in the water over the edge of the raft, while two men held us tight by the ankles, to see if the ropes on the bottom of the raft were all right.

But the ropes held. A fortnight, the seamen had said. Then all the ropes would be worn out. But in spite of this consensus of opinion we had not so far found the smallest sign of wear. Not till we were far out to sea did we find the solution. The balsa wood was so soft that the ropes wore their way slowly into the wood and were protected, instead of the logs wearing the ropes.

In calmer weather, the six sailors were able to enjoy the experience of being together on a tiny raft in the middle of the Pacific Ocean. They had taken a small dinghy and occasionally some of them would paddle away and take photographs of the raft as it was making its wonderful journey.

The raft was carried onwards. The crew realised that, without a doubt, they were being carried by winds and currents directly towards the Polynesian Islands. This thought was in their minds all the time—but there was plenty of excitement apart from this—

One night they were sleeping when . . .

About four o'clock Torstein was woken by the lamp tumbling over and something cold and wet flapping about his ears. Flying fish, he thought, and felt for it in the darkness to throw it away. He caught hold of something long and wet that wriggled like a snake, and let go as if he had burned himself. The unseen visitor twisted itself away and over to Herman, while Torstein tried to get the lamp alight. Herman started up too, and this made me wake thinking of the octopus which came up at night in these waters. When we got the lamp alight, Herman was sitting in triumph with his hand gripping the neck of a long thin fish which wriggled in his hands like an eel. The fish was over three feet long, as slender as a snake with dull black eyes and a long snout with a greedy jaw full of long sharp teeth. The teeth were as sharp as knives and could be folded back into the roof of the mouth to make way for what it swallowed.

Bengt was woken at last by all the noise, and we held the lamp and the long fish under his nose. He sat up drowsily in his sleeping bag and said solemnly:
'No fish like that don't exist.'
With which he turned over quietly and fell asleep again.
Bengt was not far wrong. It appeared later that we six sitting round the lamp in the bamboo cabin were the first men to have seen this fish alive. Only the skeleton of a fish like this one had been found a few times on the coast of South America and the Galapagos Islands.

Week followed week—but, slowly, they were coming nearer to the islands they hoped to reach.
Their excitement was great when two birds were seen. These must have flown from some island not too far distant.
Three months and two days after they had left Peru, Heyerdahl knew once and for all that his idea had worked. After years of doubt and of patience—after months at sea on a balsawood raft—this is how he heard the news:

At six o'clock Bengt came down from the masthead, woke Herman, and turned in. When Herman clambered up the creaking, swaying mast the day had begun to break. Ten minutes later he was down the rope ladder again and was shaking me by the leg.

'Come and have a look at your island!'

His face was radiant, and I jumped up, followed by Bengt, who had not quite gone to sleep yet. Hard on each other's heels, we huddled together as high as we could climb, at the point where the masts crossed. There were many birds around us, and a faint violet-blue veil over the sky was reflected in the sea as a last relic of the departing night. But over the whole horizon away to the east a ruddy glow had begun to spread, and far down to the south-east it gradually formed a blood-red background for a faint shadow, like a blue pencil line, drawn for a short way along the edge of the sea.

Land. An island.

Eventually, the raft was washed ashore on one of the Polynesian Islands—with no help from the crew. They all landed safely, and

although it had been driven on to a coral reef, even the frail balsa raft was saved from destruction.

The mast was broken and the cabin was knocked flat.

The six men remained in the islands for some time, recovering from their journey, while the whole world thrilled to the news of their adventure and admired the courage of Thor Heyerdahl and his five friends who believed in an idea enough to risk sacrificing their lives to prove that they were right.

They left for home from the island of Tahiti on board a Norwegian steamer which had changed its route to call for them.

Early one morning the big Norwegian steamer glided into Papeete harbour, and the 'Kon-Tiki' was towed out by a French naval craft to the side of her large compatriot, which swung out a huge iron arm and lifted her small kinsman up on to her deck. Loud blasts of the siren echoed over the palm-clad island. Brown and white people thronged the quay of Papeete and poured on board with farewell gifts and wreaths of flowers. We stood at the rail stretching out our necks like giraffes to get our chins free from the ever-growing load of flowers.

'If you wish yourselves back at Tahiti,' the chief Teriieroo cried as the whistle sounded over the island for the last time, 'you must throw a wreath out into the lagoon when the boat goes!'

The ropes were cast off, the engines roared, and the propeller whipped the water green as we slid sideways away from the quay.

Soon the red roofs disappeared behind the palms, and the palms were swallowed up in the blue of the mountains which sank like shadows into the Pacific.

Waves were breaking out on the blue sea. We could no longer reach down to them. White trade wind clouds drifted across the blue sky. We were no longer travelling the same way. We were defying Nature now. We were on our way to the twentieth century which lay so far, far away.

But the six of us on deck, standing beside our nine dear balsa logs, were grateful to be all alive. And in the lagoon at Tahiti six white wreaths lay alone, washing in and out, in and out with the wavelets on the beach.

Four Minute Mile

Until 1954 it was thought that no man could run one mile in less than four minutes. The greatest runners of each generation had set up new records for this distance, but the time of four minutes was believed to be the limit of human endurance.

As years went by the record came closer and closer to four minutes and one young English runner began to believe that he might be the athlete who would break this almost magic barrier. He saw this time for this distance as a challenge and was determined to succeed where so many others had failed.

Roger Bannister remembers that running had always been important to him. As a boy he was tall for his age, and slim:

As a boy I had no clear understanding of why I wanted to run. I just ran anywhere and everywhere—never because it was an end in itself, but because it was easier for me to run than to walk. My walk was ungainly, as though I had springs in my knees. I always felt impatient to see or do something new, and running saved time.

Those 'springs in his knees' were going to be very valuable to him when he grew up. But he did not always run just for pleasure—sometimes he used his skill to get away from trouble:

There was a long passage near my home patrolled by a gang of boys bigger and tougher than me. I was about eight at the time, shy, timid and easily frightened. This gang used to capture other boys and hold them in their 'den', submitting them, I imagined, to torture, the very thought of which kept me awake at night.

The threat 'snowballed' in my mind and I would walk miles to avoid this particular passage. One day I was half-way through before I thought of the danger. Then I saw the gang in a huddle. At first I tried to go on, keeping my eyes fixed on them. I felt sick with fright as I knew they were waiting for me. My steps grew more leaden, my temples pounded, my body seemed about to burst as I grew closer. I knew I ought to try to walk through, but fright won before I reached them. I turned and ran, with my head tucked down, my arms flailing vigorously. I tore round the first corner, round the second, and down the road to the safety of my home. Then a sense of shame overtook me. But I had learned the value of fright as an aid to speed.

When he left school, Bannister went to Oxford University to study medicine. His studies kept him busy, but he discovered that running was an ideal way of relaxing. Fortunately for him, there were two other students at Oxford who were just as keen on running. They were Christopher Chataway and Christopher Brasher. They became famous athletes themselves and both are well known and have appeared on television.

These two men realised that Roger Bannister would need help to run the mile faster than anyone else. They helped and encouraged him by running both with him and against him in races before the attempt on the Four Minute Mile was made.

It was a cold, bleak afternoon at the Iffley Road Track in Oxford on Thursday, May 6, 1954, when Bannister knew he had a real chance of being the first man to run 1,760 yards in less than 240 seconds. It was important for him that there should not be too much wind—this could either make running difficult or could even help so much that a record would not be recognized. To run such a race as this, an athlete's mind must be as ready as his body. Bannister had been training hard with his friends and was very fit, but the weather conditions were a real worry to him. He alone had to make the decision—would they try for the record or not?

In the afternoon, I called on Chris Chataway. At the moment the sun was shining, and he lay stretched on the window-seat. He smiled and said, just as I knew he would, 'The day could be a lot worse, couldn't it? Just now it's fine. The forecast says the wind may drop towards evening. Let's not decide until five o'clock.'

I spent the afternoon watching from the window the swaying of the leaves. 'The wind's hopeless,' said Joe Binks on the way down to the track. At 5.15 there was a shower of rain. The wind blew strongly, but now came in gusts, as if uncertain. As Brasher, Chataway and I warmed up, we knew the eyes of the spectators were on us; they were hoping the wind would drop just a little— if not enough to run a four minute mile, enough to make the attempt.

Failure is as exciting to watch as success, provided the effort is absolutely genuine and complete. But the spectators fail to understand—and how can they know—the mental agony through which an athlete must pass before he can give his maximum effort. And how rarely, if he is built as I am, he can give it.

No one tried to persuade me. The decision was mine alone, and the moment was getting closer. As we lined up for the start I glanced at the flag again. It fluttered more gently now. Yes, the wind was dropping slightly. This was the moment when I made my decision. The attempt was on.

There was complete silence on the ground . . . a false start . . . I felt angry that precious moments during the lull in the wind might be slipping by. The gun fired a second time . . . Brasher went into the lead and I slipped in effortlessly behind him, feeling tremendously full of running. My legs seemed to meet no resistance at all, as if propelled by some unknown force.

We seemed to be going so slowly. Impatiently I shouted, 'Faster!' But Brasher kept his head and did not change the pace. I went on worrying until I heard the first lap time, 57·5 sec. In my excitement my knowledge of pace had deserted me. Brasher could have run the first quarter in 55 seconds without my realising it, because I felt so full of running, but I should have had to pay for it later. Instead, he had made success possible.

At one and a half laps I was still worrying about the pace. A voice shouting 'relax' penetrated to me above the noise of the crowd . . . Unconsciously I obeyed. If the speed was wrong, it was

too late to do anything about it, so why worry? I was relaxing so much that my mind seemed almost detached from my body. There was no strain.

By now, the runners were half-way through the race. They had run twice round the quarter-mile track and there were two laps to go. Brasher was leading, Bannister was second and Chataway just behind him was third. But this was not a race against each other—it was a race against the clock. Brasher had set the pace so far. Soon it would be Chataway's turn to help . . . and then Bannister would be on his own against the seconds and fractions of seconds ticking away on the stop-watch.

I barely noticed the half-mile, passed in 1 min. 58 sec., nor when, round the next bend, Chataway went into the lead. At three-quarters of a mile the effort was still barely perceptible; the time was 3 min. 0·7 sec., and by now the crowd were roaring. Somehow I had to run that last lap in 59 seconds. Chataway led round the next bend and then I pounced past him at the beginning of the back straight, three hundred yards from the finish.

I had a moment of mixed joy and anguish, when my mind took over. It raced well ahead of my body and drew my body compellingly forward. I felt that the moment of a lifetime had come. There was no pain, only a great unity of movement and aim. The world seemed to stand still or did not exist. The only reality was the next two hundred yards of track under my feet. The tape meant finality—extinction perhaps.

I felt at that moment that it was my chance to do one thing supremely well. I drove on, impelled by a combination of fear and pride. The air I breathed filled me with the spirit of the track where I had run my first race. The noises in my ears was that of the faithful Oxford crowd. Their hope and encouragement gave me greater strength. I had now turned the last bend and there were only fifty yards more.

My body had long since exhausted all its energy, but it went on running just the same . . . this was the crucial moment when my legs were strong enough to carry me over the last few yards as they could never have done in previous years. With five yards to go the tape seemed almost to recede. Would I ever reach it?

Those last few seconds seemed never ending. The faint line of the finishing tape stood ahead as a haven of peace, after the struggle. The arms of the world were waiting to receive me if only I reached the tape without slackening my speed. If I faltered, there would be no arms to hold me and the world would be a cold, forbidding place, because I had been so close. I leapt at the tape like a man taking his last spring to save himself from the chasm that threatens to engulf him.

My effort was over and I collapsed almost unconscious, with an arm on either side of me. It was only then that the real pain overtook me. I felt like an exploded flashlight with no will to live;

45

I just went on existing in the most passive physical state without being quite unconscious. I knew that I had done it before I even heard the time. I was too close to have failed, unless my legs had played strange tricks at the finish by slowing me down and not telling my tiring brain that they had done so.

The stop-watches held the answer. The announcement came—'Result of the one mile . . . time, 3 minutes'—the rest lost in the roar of excitement. I grabbed Brasher and Chataway, and together we scampered round the track in a burst of spontaneous joy. We had done it—the three of us.

Bannister's actual time was 3 min. 59·4 sec. He ran great races after this and ran the mile in an even faster time. Since then his record has been broken by many athletes, but Roger Bannister knows that when he crossed the line in 1954, he was the FIRST to break through the barrier which men had thought to be impossible.

46

Climbing Mount Everest

London—9.30 a.m., Tuesday, June 2nd, 1953—Coronation Day
It is coronation day. The streets of London are gay with flags and decorations. All night the pavements have been packed with people —millions of men, women and children, all determined to see this historic occasion with their own eyes.

Many of the people have slept by the roadside so that they can be certain of having a good view of the Queen as she passes by.

Rain is falling, quite gently but fairly steadily, yet nothing can dampen the spirits of this mass of ordinary people who have travelled from every part of Britain—and of the world—to cheer the Queen of England on this happy day.

Suddenly there is a murmur. It seems to pass through the crowd like a breeze rustling through a field of ripe wheat. It cannot be the first signs of the procession. There are several hours to wait for that. But there is a growing, unexplained excitement. It must be something very important. Soon the murmur becomes a shout and out of the uproar these words are shouted again and again—'We've climbed Everest.'

No other news could have excited or pleased the crowd so much on this of all days. It was as if a special coronation present had been given to the Queen, and what more fitting than the conquest of the highest mountain in the world?

Before she left Buckingham Palace on that unforgettable morning, the Queen found time for one extra duty to carry out. She wrote a message to Colonel John Hunt and his expedition. Then she set out to be cheered—and crowned—and cheered again and again.

47

This is the message:

'Please convey to Col. Hunt, and all members of the British Expedition my warmest congratulations on their great achievement in reaching the summit of Mount Everest. *Elizabeth R.*'

There is something about climbing mountains which fascinates men of strength and courage. Everest—the highest and most difficult of all—was the greatest challenge. Men of many nations had tried to conquer it for years. They had spent much time, money and patience in their attempts. Other people found it difficult to understand why they did this. Sometimes the mountaineers themselves must have wondered. One of those who tried to climb Everest, a brave climber named Gordon Leigh Mallory, said that he wanted to conquer the mountain

'. . . because it was there!'

                     . . . and that was enough for him.

By the middle of the twentieth century, men who hoped to overcome the problems and dangers of such an ascent, realized that detailed planning was necessary if they were to succeed. Too many had tried, failed, and died before.

When Colonel John Hunt was asked to lead yet another expedition to Everest, he resolved to succeed—and to succeed without causing the death of any of the men who wished to accompany him.

First of all, he wanted to attract the right sort of man to share in this test of endurance and courage. Among the many men from all over the world who asked to go was a young New Zealander, Edmund Hillary. As soon as Hunt met him, he knew that here was an exceptional and dedicated man who would be valuable on any expedition, and particularly on this one. He knew that Hillary had taken part in several test climbs in the same range of mountains and that the man had the right sort of temperament and physique to help in the attempt to reach the highest peak of all.

This is what John Hunt wrote about Hillary in November 1952 just after he had met him for the first time:

Edmund Hillary, aged 33, had been a member of both "curtain-opener" expeditions, joining the first of them after he had taken part in a very successful New Zealand expedition in the Central Himalaya. Although his climbing experience dates from immediately after the war, he had quickly risen to the foremost rank among mountaineers in his own country. His testing in the Himalaya had shown that he would be a very strong contender not only for Everest, but for an eventual summit party. Quite exceptionally strong and abounding in a restless energy, possessed of a trusting mind which swept aside all unproved obstacles, Ed Hillary's personality had made its imprint on my mind, through his Cho Oyu and reconnaissance friends and through his letters to me, long before we met. He is lanky in build; by profession a bee-keeper near Auckland.

Modestly, John Hunt described himself after mentioning some of his companions on the expedition.

Lastly, there was myself. I had been climbing intermittently since 1925, when I climbed my first high Alpine peak at the age of 15. I had fitted in ten Alpine summer seasons, as well as a great deal of ski-ing. I had also done much rock climbing in this country. Owing to the fortune of being stationed in India between the wars, I had taken part in three Himalayan expeditions. I had trained troops in mountain and snow warfare, and there had been a great deal of incidental climbing in other parts of the world, made possible by military postings. I was 42.

The expedition now had a brilliant organizer and a tough mountaineer who was capable of reaching the summit. More men were needed—and one in particular . . . a man who thoroughly knew the mountains in that part of the world because he had lived in them and near them all his life.

Local men, known as 'Sherpas', would act as porters. They would be invaluable to an expedition which had the money and the organization which they lacked themselves. These Sherpas had a

feeling for the climate and the atmosphere of the land where they were born, and this the rest of the expedition lacked.

The Sherpas are hillmen whose home is in the district of Sola Khumbu in Eastern Nepal. Originally of Tibetan stock, to whose their language is closely akin, they are small sturdy men with all the sterling qualities of born mountaineers. Cheerful, loyal and courageous, possessed of exceptional hardihood, a few of them have now reached a good standard of proficiency as snow and ice climbers. They are wonderful companions on a mountain.

The Sherpas joined the Expedition when it reached Katmandu three months before the final attempt. Among them was one who stood out from the rest—Sherpa Tenzing.

His Himalayan climbing experience, and particularly his association with Everest were quite exceptional. As a young porter he had taken part in the Reconnaissance expedition of Everest in 1935, and since then he had joined the ranks of nearly every expedition to Everest. When he became one of our climbing party, he was thirty-nine, and it was his sixth visit to the mountain. We were soon firm friends. Tenzing's simplicity and gaiety quite charmed us and we were quickly impressed with his authority in the role of Sirdar (leader).

Most of John Hunt's careful planning was carried out in England. He had to ensure that oxygen would be available for the climbers to help them breathe and to maintain their strength in the thin air found at great heights. He had to test and approve every detail of clothing which his men would wear . . . to inspect tents, wireless sets, cameras and food. Here is a list of the rations, and how they were packed, which he thought would be needed by climbers if they succeeded in arriving near the summit:

MENU 7

Breakfast and March—Bottom Layer

Oatmeal Bis.	1×12 oz tin
Bacon	5×15 oz tin
Butter	2×15 oz tin
Jam	2×9 oz tin
Marmalade	2×9 oz tin
Cheese	2×8 oz tin
Choc./Sweets	$3 \times 12\frac{1}{2}$ oz tin
Salt/Matches	4 oz Salt
1 Box Matches	

Main Meal, Top Layer

Stewed Steak	8×16 oz tin
Peas	3×10 oz tin
R. Cake	4×10 oz tin

On top of tins

$2 \times 2\frac{1}{2}$ oz packets Soup powder
2 Fibre Cloths
1 packet containing Toilet paper and Can-opener

Of the hundreds of items of equipment which were provided, one proved to be very important.

Apart from the more familiar gear—thousands of feet of rope and line, pitons, snap links, ice-hammers and axes, the mountaineering equipment included certain unusual items which it seemed wise to add. We knew that, apart from crevasses of alpine dimensions, there were likely to be a few vast chasms and that these were likely to occur at the sudden change of gradient where the surface ice of the Western Cwm dips over into the Khumbu Icefall. We took a light metal 30-foot sectional ladder composed of five 6-foot lengths. It would be simple to carry and fit together and could be moved, if need be, from one crevasse to another.

The ladder proved very successful. Later, as the expedition progressed up the mountain side, it allowed the climbers to overcome major obstacles in their path in safety and with speed. This conserved much of their energy for when they needed it most—near the top.

Once the party had arrived in Nepal and had obtained permission to attempt the ascent, they began their carefully planned climb.

As they climbed higher and higher, they gradually began to realize that there was a definite chance of success. John Hunt's plans were working out—the clothes and the food, the tents and the oxygen equipment had been chosen well. Even so, it was proving to be a real test of courage, stamina and determination.

At last, they had climbed so far that they could look up and see the summit high above them.

At carefully planned intervals they left behind them Base Camps, and only a few selected members of the expedition made the final climb towards the summit.

As they climbed, these men must have thought of the others who in previous years had sought to conquer Everest and had failed. Some of these had lost their lives. Especially, they must have remembered the British climbers, Gordon Mallory and Andrew Irvine who had climbed so near the top—but who had disappeared when making their final attempt.

When John Hunt decided which men should climb to the summit he had to make a great sacrifice—to leave himself out unless it was really necessary. As leader, he was responsible for the safety of the entire expedition. Had he gone—and not returned—the lives of all the men would have been endangered. His unselfish decision ensured that he will be remembered in history as a truly great leader.

For the first attempt on the final journey to the summit, he selected Charles Evans and Tom Bourdillon. These two men all but succeeded but they wisely decided to return to the base camp when it became obvious that they did not have a certain chance of success. Had they persisted, other climbers would have been forced to risk their lives and use up precious time and supplies to set out in search of them. They, too, showed that members of a team must be unselfish and respect the demands of their final objective—in this case, to reach the top.

Next, John Hunt asked two other men to set out for the peak. He chose: Edmund Hillary and Sherpa Tenzing.

As they left their companions, they realized that this was probably the last chance which a party would have on this expedition. There were a number of minor injuries to some of the climbers and the precious supply of oxygen in the cylinders was running low.

The two men climbed as far as they could before darkness and set up a small camp as night fell. When Hillary awoke next morning he was very conscious of what he and Tenzing had to do that day. He could almost feel the good wishes of his companions coming up the mountainside towards them. He remembers every detail of the most exciting day of his life:

At 4 a.m. it was very still. I opened the tent door and looked far out across the dark and sleeping valleys of Nepal. The icy peaks below us were glowing clearly in the early morning light.

We started up our cooker and in a determined effort to prevent the weaknesses arising from dehydration we drank large quantities of lemon juice and sugar, and followed this with our last tin of sardines on biscuits. I dragged our oxygen sets into the tent, cleaned the ice off them and completely rechecked and tested them. I had removed my boots, which had become a little wet the day before, and they were now frozen solid. Drastic measures were called for, so I cooked them over the fierce fiame of the Primus and despite the very strong smell of burning leather managed to soften them up. Over our own clothing we donned our windproofs and on to our hands we pulled three pairs of gloves—silk, woollen and windproof.

At 6.30 a.m. we crawled out of our tent into the snow, hoisted our 30 lb. of oxygen gear on to our backs, connected up our masks and turned on the valves to bring life-giving oxygen into our lungs. A few deep breaths and we were ready to go.

In spite of difficulties they made good progress during the morning. At one point Hillary noticed that Tenzing was slowing up. He checked his companion's oxygen set and discovered that it had become partly blocked with ice. He cleared it and checked his own. Progress became easier again—but soon they faced their next obstacle. This was a forty foot high step of sheer rock. Normally it could have been overcome—but the climbers were tiring and time was slipping by. Hillary's keen eyes noticed a crack. He decided to make a final effort . . .

Leaving Tenzing to belay me as best he could, I jammed my way into this crack, then kicking backwards with my crampons I sank their spikes deep into the frozen snow behind me and levered myself off the ground. Taking advantage of every little rock hold and all the force of knee, shoulder and arms I could muster, I literally cramponed backwards up the crack, with a fervent prayer that the cornice would remain attached to the rock. Despite the considerable effort involved, my progress although slow was steady, and as Tenzing played out the rope I inched my way upwards until I could finally reach over the top of the rock and drag myself out of the crack on to a wide ledge.

'Crampons' or spikes attached to the soles of climbers' boots had been used with advantage by mountaineers for many years. They had never been more useful than near the top of Everest.

After a few moments rest, Hillary was ready to help Tenzing over the obstacle . . . and to move on towards the highest point in the world.

For a few moments I lay regaining my breath and for the first time really felt the fierce determination that nothing now could stop us reaching the top. I took a firm stance on the ledge and signalled to Tenzing to come on up. As I heaved hard on the rope Tenzing wriggled his way up the crack and finally collapsed exhausted at the top like a giant fish when it has just been hauled from the sea after a terrible struggle.

Their climb continued. The steep sides of the mountain, covered with hard, slippery ice still stood between them and the summit. Even Hillary began to wonder if, after all, they could still succeed.

I was beginning to tire a little now. I had been cutting steps continuously for two hours, and Tenzing, too, was moving very slowly. As I chipped steps around still another corner, I wondered rather dully just how long we could keep it up. Our original zest had now quite gone and it was turning more into a grim struggle. I then realized that the ridge ahead, instead of still monotonously rising, now dropped sharply away, and far below I could see the North Col and the Rongbuk glacier. I looked upwards to see a narrow snow ridge running up to a snowy summit. A few more whacks of the ice-axe in the firm snow and we stood on top.

. . . My initial feelings were of relief—relief that there were no more steps to cut—no more ridges to traverse and no more humps to tantalize us with hopes of success. I looked at Tenzing and in spite of the balaclava, goggles and oxygen mask all encrusted with long icicles that concealed his face, there was no disguising his infectious grin of pure delight as he looked all around him. We shook hands and then Tenzing threw his arm around my shoulders and we thumped each other on the back until we were almost breathless. It was 11.30 a.m. The ridge had taken us two and a half hours, but it seemed like a lifetime. I turned off the oxygen and removed my set. I had carried my camera, loaded with colour film, inside my shirt to keep it warm, so I now produced it and got Tenzing to pose on top for me, waving his axe on which was a string of flags—United Nations, British, Nepalese and Indian.

For ten short minutes, Hillary gazed around him at the spectacular view. He took a few more photographs and then realized that, without oxygen, he was beginning to feel weak. Quickly, he replaced his oxygen set and looked to see what his companion was doing.

Meanwhile, Tenzing had made a little hole in the snow and in it he placed various small articles of food—a bar of chocolate, a packet of biscuits and a handful of lollies. Small offerings, indeed, but at least a token gift to the Gods that all devout Buddhists believe have their home on this lofty summit. While we were together on the South Col two days before, Hunt had given me a small crucifix which he had asked me to take to the top. I, too, made a hole in the snow and placed the crucifix beside Tenzing's gifts.

I checked our oxygen once again. We would have to move fast in order to reach our life-saving reserve below the South Peak. After fifteen minutes we turned to go. We looked briefly for any signs of Mallory and Irvine, but had seen nothing.

The journey back to the Base Camp IV was not easy but the climbers were spurred on by their success. They were impatient to tell their news to one man—John Hunt.

We had reached the top.

To see the unashamed joy spread over the tired, strained face of our gallant and determined leader was to me reward enough in itself.

This was the news which reached London four days later—and the whole world joined in the cheering!

Anne's Diary

Many children at school start their day by writing their Daily Diaries. Usually they write about their family and friends, about where they have been the day before, about events in school—or even about news which has happened recently in the rest of the world.

Diaries are always interesting to read, years after they are written, and often the greater the number of years—the greater is their interest.

One of the most famous history books ever written was actually a secret diary written in code by a man named Samuel Pepys. His eyewitness accounts of important events in the Seventeenth Century tell us more than any other book about the Great Plague, the Great Fire of London and life in London during the reign of Charles II. Captain Scott's Diary is our only record of his terrible march to and from the South Pole.

During the Second World War, one schoolgirl spent many hours writing in her diary.

She enjoyed writing—but her diary became more important than almost anything else in her life for a special reason. In many ways it is one of the saddest and most interesting diaries ever written.

This young girl, Anne Frank, was not able to leave her home during the years when the diary was written. She was quite fit, she wanted to go out—and yet although she had done nothing wrong, had committed no crime, she was imprisoned in a small room, hidden away from the world outside.

In 1940 the Germans invaded and quickly conquered the country of Holland together with most of the other countries in Europe.

At this time, the German leaders were cruel, unreasonable men with strange and terrible ideas. One of these ideas was that all Jews were evil and should be killed—or at least imprisoned in great Concentration Camps where they suffered greatly and where many hundreds of thousands died.

Anne Frank's parents were Jews. They were Germans who had fled from Hitler's Germany in 1933 to seek safety in Holland. Now that the Germans ruled Holland, Anne's family was in even greater danger. Soon after the German invasion had taken place, Anne's father decided that he must find a hiding place for his wife, his two daughters and for a few of his Jewish friends so that the Germans would not be able to find them and take them away.

By June, 1942 the Germans were looking for them. Anne had lived for nearly two years under the German occupation. She had been forced to wear a yellow star on her clothes to show she was Jewish. She was not allowed to ride a bicycle, to travel in a tram or to enter a cinema.

Her father was able to prepare two large rooms at the top of an old block of offices. The narrow entrance to the rooms was hidden by a moveable bookcase. Behind this strange door, the following people lived for two years:

Anne Frank, Margot Frank (Anne's 16 year old sister), Mr. & Mrs. Frank, Mr. & Mrs. Van Daan, Peter Van Daan (aged 15), a man called Dussel, a dentist.

Friday, June 12th, 1942 was Anne Frank's 13th birthday. She had not yet entered her secret hiding place. She was very pleased with her presents and like most girls of her age she made a careful list of everything which she was given. Among her gifts were flowers, chocolates, a brooch, a party game, some money, two books . . . and an empty diary.

For her first entry, she wrote a message—to the diary itself. It was almost as if she was being introduced to a friend who would be very important to her. This is what the first page looked like when she put her diary away at the end of her birthday:

This message is written in Dutch—but these are the words she wrote

Ik zal hoop ik aan jou alles kunnen
toevertrouwen, zoals ik het nog aan
niemand gekund heb, en ik hoop dat
ji mi grote steun voor me zult zijn.
Anne Frank, 12 Juni 1942.

I hope I shall be able to confide in you completely, as I have
never been able to do in anyone before, and I hope that you will be
a great support and comfort to me.

Anne Frank, 12th June, 1942

When she wrote these words, it was as if Anne Frank had been
given a glimpse of the future, for indeed, her diary really was
destined to be what she hoped—'a great support and comfort to
her.'

She had just one month of freedom left to her. In those last days
before she went into hiding her diary tells of the same kind of events
that happen to all teen-age girls—her friendships, her examination
results, her fondness for Ping-Pong—and ice-creams. Anne was one
of those girls who loved talking—even when she was in the class-
room! She tells how one of her teachers punished her for this by
making her write a composition entitled 'Incurable Chatterbox.'
Even this did not stop her and next she had to write another with the
strange title 'Quack, Quack, Quack says Mrs. Natterbeak.' With a
friend's help, Anne wrote her punishment essay as a poem. Her
teacher was pleased with the result. He read it to the whole class and
to other classes in the school as well.

But really, writing stories and essays and poems was no punishment for her. She loved writing as much as she loved talking.

Her examination results were good and she was very pleased with
herself when she recorded them in her diary. She was not so pleased
when she had to recall a visit to the dentist, on a very hot day—

especially as she had to walk a long way as she was not allowed to ride on a tram because she was Jewish ... 'Shanks's pony is good enough for us.'

By now, her diary had become as important to her as a friend. She had given this friend a name—'Kitty' and most of her entries are like letters. They begin with these words: *Dear Kitty*.

Suddenly her whole life was changed. On Sunday, July 15th, 1942 she wrote:

Dear Kitty,

Our examination results were announced last Friday. I couldn't have hoped for better. My report is not at all bad. They were certainly pleased at home, although over the question of marks my parents are different from most. They don't care a bit as long as I'm well and happy, and not too cheeky. I am just the opposite. I don't want to be a bad pupil. My sister Margot has her report too, brilliant as usual. She is so brainy.

A few days ago, Daddy began to talk of going into hiding. I asked him why on earth he was beginning to talk of that already. 'Yes, Anne,' he said, 'you know we have been taking food, clothes, furniture to other people for over a year now. We don't want our belongings to be seized by the Germans, and we certainly don't want to fall into their clutches ourselves. So we shall disappear of our own accord and not wait until they come to fetch us.'

'But Daddy, when would it be?' He spoke so seriously that I grew very anxious.

'Don't worry about it, we shall arrange everything. Make the most of your carefree young life while you can.' That was all.

Yours, Anne

Events moved quickly. There is an urgency about the next entry in her journal, written only three days later.

Wednesday, 8th July, 1942

Dear Kitty,

Years seem to have passed between Sunday and now. So much has happened, it is just as if the whole world has turned upside down. But I am still alive, Kitty, and that is the main thing, Daddy says.

I will begin by telling you what happened on Sunday afternoon.

At three o'clock someone rang the front door bell. A bit later, Margot appeared at the kitchen door looking very excited. 'The S.S. have sent a call-up notice for Daddy,' she whispered. 'Mummy has gone to see Mr. Van Daan already.' (Van Daan is a friend who works with Daddy in business.) It was a great shock to me, a call-up; everyone knows what that means.

Suddenly the bell rang again. We heard Mummy and Mr. Van

Daan downstairs talking then they came in and closed the door behind them. Van Daan wanted to talk to Mummy alone. When we were together in our bedroom, Margot told me that the call up was not for Daddy—but for her. I was more frightened than ever and began to cry. Margot is sixteen; would they really take girls of that age away? But thank goodness she will not go. Mummy said so herself; that must be what Daddy said when he talked about us going into hiding.

Into hiding—where would we go, in a town or the country, in a house or a cottage, when, how, where . . . ?

These were the questions I was not allowed to ask, but I couldn't get them out of my mind. Margot and I began to pack some of our most vital belongings into a school satchel. The first thing I put in was this diary, then hair curlers, handkerchiefs, school books, a comb, old letters; I put in the craziest things with the idea that we were going into hiding. But I'm not sorry, memories mean more to me than dresses.

The very next day she went into hiding—

We walked in the pouring rain, Daddy, Mummy and I each with a school satchel and shopping bag filled to the brim, with all kinds of things thrown together anyhow.

We got sympathetic looks from people on their way to work. You could see by their faces how sorry they were they couldn't offer us a lift; the gaudy yellow star spoke for itself.

During the walk to the hiding place, Anne's parents explained how they had been planning this secret sanctuary for months. It was very ingenious. Anne tells 'Kitty' about every detail. She explains that the building to which they were going was one of many office blocks by the side of a canal. To reach their secret home, a visitor would have to enter a large warehouse, go through an office, climb several staircases and pass through many doors. The actual entrance to the Frank's new home was concealed by a bookcase containing ordinary files and books which were similar to those in thousands of other offices in the city.

Settling in took some time. There was a great deal of tidying up to do in order to make the rooms habitable for the large number of

people who were going to live there.

By August 14th, Anne had become accustomed to her new life ... and she was beginning to feel bored with her strange existence. Of course, it helped to tell 'Kitty' all about it:

Friday, 14th August, 1942

Dear Kitty,

I have deserted you for a whole month, but honestly there is so little news here that I can't find amusing things to tell you every day. The Van Daans arrived on July 13th. We thought they were coming on the 14th, but between the 13th and the 16th of July the Germans called up more people right and left which created more and more unrest, so they played for safety. Better a day too early than a day too late.

It is not difficult to imagine how the inhabitants of this unusual prison irritated each other before long. In particular, Anne began to lose patience with the second housewife in their home, Mrs. Van Daan:

Monday, 21st September, 1942

Dear Kitty,

Today I'm going to tell you our general news.

Mrs. Van Daan is unbearable. I get nothing but 'Blowings up' from her for my continuous chatter. She is always pestering us in some way or another. This is the latest: she doesn't want to wash up the pans if a tiny bit is left; instead of putting it in a glass dish, as we've always done until now, she leaves it in the pan to go bad.

After the next meal Margot sometimes has about seven pans to wash up and then Madame says: 'Well, well, Margot, you HAVE got a lot to do.'

I had just written something about Mrs. Van Daan when in she came. Slap! I closed the book.

'Hey, Anne, can't I just have a look?'

'I'm afraid not.'

'Just the last page then?'

'No, I'm sorry.'

Naturally it gave me a frightful shock, because there was an unflattering description of her on that particular page.

Yours, Anne.

It was natural for a young girl to feel resentful of strangers in her own home—but the specially difficult conditions under which they lived created situations where she felt that even her own family were at fault. It was as well that 'Kitty' was—as always—ready to listen without answering back . . .

Saturday, 7th November 1942

Dear Kitty,

Mummy is frightfully irritable and that always seems to herald unpleasantness for me. Is it just chance that Daddy and Mummy never rebuke Margot and that they always drop on me for everything? Yesterday evening, for instance: Margot was reading a book with lovely drawings in it; she got up and went upstairs, put the book down ready to go on with later. I wasn't doing anything, so picked up the book and started looking at the pictures. Margot came back, saw 'her' book in my hands, wrinkled her forehead and asked for the book back. Just because I wanted to look a little farther on, Margot got more and more angry. Then Mummy joined in: 'Give the book to Margot; she was reading it,' she said. Daddy came into the room. He didn't even know what it was all about, but saw the injured look on Margot's face and promptly dropped on me: 'I'd like to see what you would say if Margot ever started looking at one of your books.' I gave way at once, laid the book down and left the room—offended as they thought. It so happened that I was neither offended nor cross, just miserable. It wasn't right of Daddy to judge without knowing what the squabble was about. I would have given Margot the book myself, and much more quickly, if Mummy and Daddy hadn't interfered. They took Margot's part at once.

Yours, Anne

If you were forced to live as Anne Frank had to live, you would realize how important unimportant events become—even the loss of a fountain pen.

It was on a Friday afternoon after five o'clock. I had come out of my room to go and sit at the table to write, when I was roughly pushed on one side and had to make room for Margot and Daddy who wanted to practise their 'Latin'. The fountain pen remained on the table, unused while, with a sigh, its owner contented herself with a tiny little corner of the table and started rubbing beans.

'Bean rubbing' is making mouldy beans decent again. I swept the floor at a quarter to six and threw the dirt, together with the bad beans, into a newspaper and into the stove. A terrific flame leapt out and I thought it was grand that the fire should burn up so well when it was practically out.

First Anne, then the whole family began to search for the missing pen. It was nowhere to be found. Her sister suggested that it had fallen into the stove together with the beans . . .

And so it was that our unhappy fears were confirmed; when Daddy did the stove the following morning the clip used for fastening was found among the ashes. Not a trace of the gold nib was found. 'Must have melted and stuck to some stone or other,' Daddy thought.

Gradually the confinement of her secret home had its effect on Anne. In the winter all of us look forward to the spring. For Anne, spring meant so much more—even if she was not able to go out and enjoy the excitement of the new season and its awakening. Her diary entry at this time has a hint of poetry about it:

Saturday, 12th February, 1944

Dear Kitty,
The sun is shining, the sky is a deep blue, there is a lovely breeze and I'm longing—so longing—for everything. To talk, for freedom, for friends, to be alone. And I do so long . . . to cry! I feel as if I'm going to burst, and I know that it would be better with crying; but I can't, I'm restless, I go from one room to the other, breathe through the crack of a closed window, feel my heart beating, as if it is saying, 'Can't you satisfy my longings at last?'

I believe that it's spring within me, I feel that spring is awakening, I feel it in my whole body and soul. It is an effort to behave normally, I feel confused, don't know what to read, what to write, what to do, I only know I am longing . . . !

Yours, Anne

Months passed and became a year—then two years. Anne's diary was filling up. Yet again, she seemed to sense that it would be read long after the war and that it would be of interest to those who lived after her.

Wednesday, 29th March, 1944

Dear Kitty,
Bolkestein, a Minister, was speaking on the Dutch programme from London, and he said that they ought to make a collection of diaries and letters after the war. Of course they all made a rush at my diary immediately. Just imagine how interesting it would be if I were to publish a romance of the 'Secret Annexe'. The title

alone would be enough to make people think it was a detective story.

But seriously, it would seem quite funny ten years after the war if we Jews were able to tell how we lived and what we ate and talked about here. Although I tell you a lot, still, even so, you only know very little of our lives.

All the time the world outside the 'prison' was catching up with her. The prisoners in that small attic heard occasional news of the world outside. Anne and her family and friends were thrilled when Allied troops landed in France on D Day in June, 1944 to begin the liberation of Europe. They really began to believe that their nightmare existence would be over before long—but Normandy in France was a long way from Amsterdam in Holland and friendly troops did not advance quickly enough to save all the inhabitants of the countries like Holland who were praying and hoping for their freedom again.

Just as it seemed that the war would be over, the Germans occupying Holland seemed to speed up their attacks on the Jews. Anne knew about some of these and although she believed that these things could not happen to her or her family the news was upsetting to her.

Thursday, 25th May, 1944

Dear Kitty,

This morning our vegetable man was picked up for having two Jews in his house. It's a great blow to us, not only that those poor Jews are balancing on the edge of an abyss, but it's terrible for the man himself.

The world has turned topsy-turvy, respectable people are being sent off to concentration camps, prisons and lonely cells. One person walks into the trap through the black market, a second through helping the Jews or other people who've had to go 'underground.'

This man is a great loss to us too—the only thing to do is to eat less. I will tell you how we shall do that; Mummy says we shall cut out breakfast altogether, have porridge and bread for lunch, and for supper fried potatoes and possibly once or twice per week vegetables or lettuce, nothing more. We're going to be hungry, but anything is better than being discovered.

Yours, Anne

On Tuesday, 1st August, 1944, Anne wrote a longer entry than usual. She was trying to find a way of living which would be acceptable to everybody—to her parents, her sister, to her friends and to herself:

. . . I keep on trying to find a way of becoming what I would so like to be, and what I could be, if . . . there weren't any other people living in the world.

Yours Anne

Those were the last words she wrote. We know that three days later the secret annexe was discovered by the Police. All who lived there were taken away. Anne never saw her parents again. Together with her sister Margot, she was taken to the terrible camp at Belsen in Germany. Just a few weeks before the camp was liberated by Allied soldiers, Anne and her sister died.

But Anne's thoughts and ideas lived on in the pages of her own secret diary. This was found buried in a pile of newspapers in the attic in Amsterdam and given to her father after the war. He was the only inhabitant of the secret annexe to survive. Many books have been written about the war—and about the strange, age old persecution of the Jews—by generals, politicians, soldiers and priests, on both sides and by the ordinary men and women of the countries which took part. Yet this diary of an ordinary schoolgirl seems to say more about the evils of war, and of racial persecution, than any other writing—and in a unique way.

Anne Frank was innocent of any crime. She wanted to live. Perhaps she was more than an ordinary schoolgirl, because her story has been read by millions of people after her life ended when she was so young. Her diary is a powerful argument against the persecution of human beings because they happen to be of a certain race or colour—and Anne's dearest wish is fulfilled every time her words are read by men and women and children of every nation—and by you, today:

74

I want to go on living after my death. And therefore I am grateful to God for giving me this gift . . . of expressing all that is within me.

The Man
who walked
... in Space

If you lift something heavy and then let it go, it will fall to the ground. Anyone will tell you that it falls because the force of gravity is pulling it towards the centre of the earth.

It is this force which MAKES things fall—and it is this force which prevents human beings from flying—unless we can overcome the pull of gravity by using an engine or machine.

Men have been trying to overcome this 'pull' since earliest times. You will probably know the story of Daedalus and his son, Icarus, who, according to the ancient Greeks, made wings for themselves so that they could fly like birds. Their wings were made of wax and feathers. The legend tells us that the wax melted when they flew close to the sun and that Icarus fell into the sea and was drowned. Although this IS a legend, it proves that even the peoples of the oldest civilizations were planning to fly ... to overcome the force of gravity.

The first successful attempt to overcome the pull of gravity was made with a 'lighter than air' balloon made by the Montgolfier brothers in France rose in the air in 1783.

The next real success was achieved by the Wright brothers of America who used the principles of flight to propel a 'heavier than air' machine above the earth in 1903 at Kitty Hawk in North Carolina.

Since then, aeroplanes have become commonplace. Many ordinary people have flown in aeroplanes and there can be few people alive who have not seen an aeroplane in flight high above the earth.

During the Second World War another way of overcoming

gravity was perfected. This used the principle of the 'thrust' achieved by a 'rocket.'

Giant rockets (using highly specialized and powerful fuels) were made to shoot high into the sky. Because it was wartime these rockets contained bombs in their noses. When they fell, they exploded—and because of the speed and height which they reached, it was impossible to stop them. Fortunately, they were not used until near the end of the war and their real powers of destruction were never fully used.

Out of this discovery in the war, grew an exciting development in peace. The most powerful nations, Russia and America, determined to develop the rockets so that, eventually, they could send them high enough into the sky to escape the force of gravity.

This meant designing rockets powerful enough to thrust away from the earth's surface so that they (and anything which they carried) would float around the earth in orbit.

The Russians were the first to place an object in space. In 1957 they put *Sputnik One* into orbit around the earth and this tiny satellite relayed information back to them.

Next, the Russians sent living things into space. First, two dogs —then, at last, a MAN, Yuri Gagarin in 1961. The dogs died painlessly in their capsules after their reactions to space travel had proved that animal life could survive there. But, if you send a MAN into space, you must be sure that you know how to return him safely to earth.

This 're-entry' into the earth's atmosphere is achieved by using small rockets which force the capsule back until it is again affected by pull of gravity so that it falls to the earth. By using devices such as 'retro-rockets' and parachutes, scientists are able to do this without destroying the capsule—or killing the astronaut. Yet there are many difficulties. The capsule could hurtle towards the earth and smash against its surface—or it could burn up as it fell at tremendous speed through the atmosphere where the friction created would reduce it (and its occupants) to a cinder.

Yuri Gagarin returned safely and won a special place in history as the first man to go into space. He saw the world as it had never been seen before. Once this milestone had been passed, other human beings followed him. Russian men (and a woman) made space flights—so did many Americans.

The scientists and space pioneers were not satisfied with these miraculous achievements which had seemed unbelievable only a few years earlier. They were encouraged by their success to go further.

Two astronauts were sent up together—then three. Space vehicles were linked up while in orbit. Records for length of time in space were set up—and then broken. Next, men turned their attention to the earth's own natural satellite—the Moon. They carried out many brilliant and successful experiments with amazing success with the idea of landing men on this bleak world in space. Capsules crashed on to its surface—sending radio signals back to earth until the very moment of impact—when the moon's own 'pull' drew the capsules to it's surface and destroyed them. Next, capsules went into orbit AROUND the moon itself and sent signals back to earth with new information about the moon. Only parts of the moon can be seen through the powerful telescopes of astronomers so the next step was to send television cameras in space vehicles which made 'soft landings' on to the moon and to relay close-up pictures of its surface. Soon, a mechanical arm was built into one of these devices and our knowledge of the moon's surface became so complete, that it was clear that men could survive there for a limited space of time.

In spite of this quest to reach the moon, other places in the Solar System were explored. Mars and Venus (our nearest neighbours among the planets) received visits from objects sent by earth.

Yet, in the minds of Russian and American scientists, the main objective is still to land men on the moon and to bring them safely back to earth. Events have moved so quickly in the short history of space travel that it is difficult for us to say: 'That was an historic moment'—even when we hear of yet another remarkable achievement.

What sort of people are the astronauts themselves? They are just as brave and adventurous as the men who have explored the remotest parts of the earth. Like Scott and Hillary they have the urge to be the 'first' in places where man has not been before. Like Bannister and Heyerdahl, they long to prove a scientific principle—

even at the risk of their own lives. In spite of the rapid and ambitious progress in space exploration, there have been no casualties away from our own planet . . . out in the emptiness of space—although several astronauts have died while testing equipment or while returning to the earth itself.

The programme of a space flight is complicated and highly organized. Gradually ordinary people have been able to see and hear what happens by watching television or by listening to the radio. Indeed, space flights have become so common—and scientific developments so successful—that even LIVE television transmissions from space itself are now possible.

Millions of ordinary people were able to share in one of the most remarkable space flights which has ever taken place . . . and were able to follow the whole operation as it happened.

James McDivitt   *Edward White*

79

This mission was known as *Gemini IV*—the fourth flight in a whole series given the name *Gemini* by the Americans. Their first series was called *Project Mercury* and the third, *Project Apollo*. When *Apollo* has been completed, it is hoped that men will have been placed on the moon and will have been returned safely to earth again.

Gemini IV began long before the date of launching. The two astronauts for the mission had been selected nearly a year earlier. Both were expert pilots and both had to be in perfect physical condition. Both had undergone a long and difficult training in the control of a space capsule and in how to manage weightlessness. This weightlessness is the result of being free from the pull of gravity. A man in space cannot 'fall'—he floats and even has to be secured within his tiny cabin.

For astronauts James McDivitt and Edward White, June 3rd, 1965 was the date which was the most important in their lives. High on the top of a huge Titan rocket was the tiny capsule which was to be their home in space.

About five hours before the launch, the two men were awakened. An hour later they were eating breakfast. Forty minutes later they had put on their elaborate space suits.

The task given to astronaut McDivitt was a difficult one. He was to be the pilot of the *Gemini IV* capsule. He would have to take over the controls once the rocket had fallen away and the capsule itself was in space. He was to control it during the flight and, acting on detailed instructions from the Gemini Control Centre, was to guide the capsule back through the earth's atmosphere until it made a safe landing in the sea.

Astronaut White's task was a shorter one—but even more demanding. He had been instructed to attempt a 'space-walk'— outside the capsule itself. For months he had been training in a special room learning how to guide himself with a new invention— a 'space gun'.

The hundreds of scientists and technicians concerned with the project became more and more excited as the time for the launch drew nearer. Indeed, McDivitt and White looked calmer than any of them as they walked to Launching Pad 19 at Cape Kennedy in their heavy space suits. They were taken to the top of the giant rocket in a lift. They entered the capsule and settled into a reclining position ready for the launch. As the hatches were closed over them they must have felt very isolated. Except for the astronauts themselves, everybody left the launching site.

From the blockhouse where the launching control was situated hundreds of eyes were on the rocket and the giant tower which held it upright. But from the rocket and the tiny spacecraft on its tip no movement could be seen.

Millions of listeners the world over could hear the tension in voices of the controllers. Seconds before 11.16 Eastern Daylight

Time on that sunny June morning, the final orders were given. Clouds of vapour began to pour from the lower end of the rocket— it began to lift vertically into the air. Another space adventure had begun.

For those on the ground it must have seemed very quiet as the Titan rocket disappeared high above the earth. Everyone relaxed. Blast-off had been successful. Soon the rocket had parted from the capsule and Gemini Four was in orbit round the earth. Until McDivitt fired the retro-rockets it would continue in the same orbit —100 miles at its nearest point to the earth and 175 miles farthest out.

Up in the tiny capsule, the two astronauts relaxed as well. Although there were tremendous risks still to come, they felt that now the actual launch was over their mission would be successful.

Four hours later the tension began again. Down in the Gemini Control Centre at Houston in Texas, one of the commentators announced the next development.

A message had been received via the island of Hawaii where McDivitt's voice had been heard from far out in space.

Gemini Control: 'This is Gemini Control. 4 hours and 24 minutes into the mission. The Hawaii station has just established contact and the pilot, Jim McDivitt, advises the cabin has been depressurised. It is reading zero. We are standing by for a GO from Hawaii to open the hatch. . . . White has opened the door. He has stood up, and it's a most relaxed period. McDivitt reports that White is standing on the seat . . . '

Capsule Communicator, Hawaii: 'All systems on the ground look good . . . '

Flight Director, Houston: 'You're having him get out?'

Capsule Communicator: 'Roger, Flight, we're GO . . . '

Flight Director: 'Tell him we're ready to have him get out when he is.'

Capsule Communicator to Gemini: 'We just had word from Houston we're ready to have you get out whenever you're ready. Give us a mark when you egress the spacecraft . . . '

Gemini: 'He's ready to egress right now.'

And Astronaut White stepped out of the spacecraft. Although there was no sensation of speed, White was actually travelling at a speed (in relation to the surface of the earth) of 5 miles PER SECOND.

White's life depended upon remaining attached to the capsule. To have lost contact with it would have meant that he would have floated away . . . far into space with no hope of returning to earth. He was attached to the capsule by a 'tether'—a twenty-five foot long gold plated tube which passed oxygen to him from the capsule and which contained wires to carry his voice from outside to inside the capsule . . . and then back to earth. The tube was covered with a nylon rope capable of taking a strain of over 1,000 pounds.

This 'tether' was important—but another piece of equipment was of great interest to Gemini Control. It was called the 'Manoeuvring Unit.' This was what the astronauts called the 'space gun.' When the trigger was pulled, a jet of gas shot out and allowed White to move in the direction he wanted.

On earth, the team at Gemini IV Control sat silent as they heard the voices from space. White was able to speak by radio from outside the capsule and his words and descriptions were heard all over the earth as he spoke.

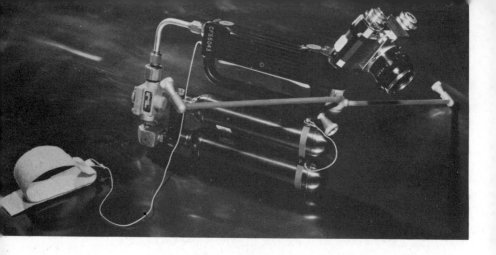

Gemini Control: 'This is Gemini Control, Houston. Gus Grissom has just established contact with the spacecraft. McDivitt confirms that White did leave the spacecraft. He said he looks great. He's outside working his manoeuvring unit and Jim is quite exuberant about the performance that he's witnessing at this time. Let's cut in live now and listen to what White says . . .'

White: 'The manoeuvring unit is good. The only problem I have is that I haven't got enough fuel. I've exhausted the fuel now and I was able to manoeuvre myself down to the bottom of the spacecraft and I was right up on top of the adapter . . . I'm looking right down and it looks like we're coming up on the coast of California, and I'm going in slow rotation to the right.'

McDivitt: 'One thing about it, when Ed gets out there and starts whipping around it sure makes the spacecraft difficult to control . . .'

White: 'I'm going to work on getting some pictures, Jim . . .'

McDivitt: 'O.K. Get out in front where I can see you again . . . Where are you?'

White: 'Right out in front now. I don't have the control I had any more . . . There's no difficulty in recontacting the spacecraft . . .' particularly in trying to move back . . . I'm very thankful in having the experience to be first . . .'

McDivitt: 'Ed, will you please roll around? Right now we're just about pointing straight down to the ground.'

White: 'O.K., now I'm taking a look back at the adapter. I'm looking back there. The thrusters are clean. The sun in space is not blinding but it's quite nice. I'm coming back down on the spacecraft. I can sit out here and see the whole California coast.'

Flight Surgeon: 'Flight, this is Surgeon. The data looks great here.'

Flight Director: 'How's his E.C.G.?' (Electrocardiogram—a machine used to measure heart beat).

Flight Surgeon: 'It looks great, Flight. He's just ripping along here at a great rate.'

McDivitt: 'You smeared up my windshield, you dirty dog! You see how it's all smeared up there?'

White: 'Yep!'

McDivitt: 'Looks like there's a coating on the outside and you've rubbed it off. That's apparently what you've done.'

We know exactly what White must have looked like from inside the spacecraft:

Two cameras were photographing him as he floated around. One was a motion film camera and the other was operated by the pilot, astronaut McDivitt who found time to take photographs as well as to control the spacecraft! He took this photograph of White—and the earth can be seen in the background.

The experimental space gun was very successful—but White enjoyed walking in space so much that he stayed outside longer than he should have done and used up all the fuel which the gun contained. However, by pulling on his nylon tether, he was able to move where he wanted—and he, too, found time to use his camera to photograph the earth and to take pictures of a spacecraft in orbit for the very first time—from space itself.

Gemini Control became alarmed. White had stayed outside longer than had been intended. Capsule Communicator's voice became stern:

Capsule Communicator: 'Gemini IV. Tell him the flight director says to get back in.

McDivitt: 'O.K. Yeh, well get back in. You have three and a half more days to go buddy ... do you hear that, Ed? ... Get back in.'

White: 'I'm on top of it right now.'

McDivitt: 'O.K. You're right on top. Come on in then ... '

White: 'All right. I'm coming, boy, I'm coming.'
McDivitt: 'I'll put the gun up.'
White: 'I'll open the door and come through there.'
McDivitt: 'O.K. Let's not lose this camera now. I don't quite have
it. A little bit more. O.K. I've got it . . . Come on, Let's get back
in here before it gets dark.'

Altogether, White had been outside in space for 21 minutes. He
had proved many things. Man could live in space. He could manoeuvre. He could perform tasks (such as taking photographs) and
thus could (in the future) transfer from one space vehicle to another
—or assemble a Space Station—or repair or make adjustments to
unmanned satellites in space.

McDivitt and White still had much to do. They circled the earth
59 more times after the space walk. Eventually, Gemini Control
gave instructions to return to earth. The 'retro-rockets' were fired.
The spacecraft re-entered the earth's atmosphere. There was a
successful 'splashdown' in the Pacific Ocean close to the waiting
Aircraft Carrier, U.S.S. *Wasp*. The astronauts were transferred to
an inflatable dinghy. Naval frogmen placed a 'flotation collar'

around the capsule which was eventually picked up and taken to the
Wasp. White and McDivitt were taken by helicopter to the aircraft
carrier and received a hero's welcome aboard. They had been
in space for 97 hours and 56 minutes.

Later, White talked about his Space Walk. Here are some of his
comments:

'There was absolutely no sensation of falling. There was very
little sensation of speed, other than the same type of sensation
that we had in the capsule, and I would say that it would be very
similar to flying over the earth from about 20,000 feet. You can't
actually see the earth moving underneath you . . . I think as I
stepped out, I thought probably the biggest thing was the feeling
of accomplishment of one of the goals of the Gemini IV mission.
I think that was probably in my mind. I think that is as close as I
can give it to you.'

'The tether was quite useful. I was able to go right back where I
started every time, but I wasn't able to manoeuvre specific points
with it. Another use of the tether that Jim mentioned to me was

that I also used it to pull myself down to the spacecraft, and at one time I called down and said, "I'm actually walking across the top of the spacecraft," and that is exactly what I was doing.'

'We were looking to find out, could man control himself in space—and the answer is "Yes, man can control himself in space." He needs a little more fuel than was provided to me.'

There was still a great deal of work for everyone connected with Gemini Four. The capsule itself was extremely important. Every inch was examined by experts. They were pleased to see how well the spacecraft had stood up to the heat caused by the re-entry into the earth's atmosphere. The effects of the heat caused by friction can be seen clearly on the base of the capsule.

Astronauts White and McDivitt were given a long medical examination and they had to answer hundreds of questions. After this, they were free to go—first to meet the President of the United States and then to be re-united with their families.

For most men, this experience would have satisfied any longings to be pioneers in space. It would have been enough to settle back and bask in the glory of their achievements—but both astronauts asked to continue as members of America's space team. Their experience was invaluable to those who plan future space projects.

Astronaut White took part in further tests on the ground at Cape Kennedy. As the first American to experience 'Extra-Vehicular Activity,' he was assigned to the *Apollo* mission—which aims to put men on the moon.

Early in 1967, while testing an Apollo moonshot spacecraft on the ground, there was a 'flash-fire.' White and his two companions were killed instantly. His bravery and the adventurous spirit in his heart will continue to inspire future space experiments . . . and Astronaut White takes his place in history among those men who long to extend our knowledge of the world—and of the universe itself.

Votes for Women

For at least one day each year you are not allowed to go to school. This has nothing to do with holidays. It is because your school is being used as a polling station.

This means that men and women go to your school to vote for the person they would like to represent them as a councillor on their local council. Once every five years (at least) they vote to choose the man or woman they want to represent their own area (or Constituency) as a Member of Parliament in the House of Commons at Westminster.

If you happen to be near your school on one of these Election Days, you will see many men and women making their way to the special booths inside so that they can put X against the name of the candidate they prefer. Usually, the polling stations are busiest in the evenings when the men have come home from work. Husbands and wives may go together to cast their votes.

This is a common sight nowadays but it was not always so. Not very long ago women were not allowed to vote. Thousands of brave women put up with ridicule and suffering because they believed that husbands and wives, that men and women should have a say in the government of their town and their country.

Strangely enough, it was a woman who had ruled Great Britain for the second half of the Nineteenth Century. Under Queen Victoria, Britain had won a vast Empire and over a quarter of the inhabitants of the world were her subjects. As Queen of England, and Empress of India, she ruled her dominions through a Parliament elected by men and in which only men were allowed to serve.

For centuries women had left the government of their country to men. The idea of women voting to select the members of the government was unthinkable. The idea of women themselves taking part in that government seemed ridiculous.

The death of Queen Victoria in 1901 was seen by the world as the end of an age. A king (Edward VII) came to the throne. Changes had to come and all over the world men and women began to think about the opportunities for a new life in the new Twentieth Century. Motor cars had already been invented. The first aeroplane would soon be flying. Machines were becoming more efficient and ingenious. Education was there for everybody and ordinary people were being taught to think for themselves.

It was realised that there were many injustices. First, there was a great difference between rich and poor. Unless a man was fortunate enough to be born into a fairly rich family he could not expect to become more than a poorly paid worker—however clever he might be.

Soon women realised that they should be taken seriously and have a say in the government of their country. Up to now they had not counted for much and even such authors as George Eliot and the Brontë sisters had to adopt male pen names in order to have their books published. Intelligent women knew that they had no say in the government while men, however dull or stubborn or unintelligent they might be, looked upon this as their right—simply because they were men.

One woman who thought about this was Emmeline Pankhurst. She was born in 1858 and was 43 when Queen Victoria died. More fortunate than most, she had been born into a well-to-do Manchester family and received a good education. Her father possessed a fine library and Emmeline was a great reader. What she read made her think—and after her marriage to Dr. Richard Pankhurst, she went on thinking, encouraged by her husband who hoped to enter parliament. It is likely that he would have become an M.P.—had it not been for just one idea in which he believed very strongly. This idea frightened the politicians of the time and Dr. Pankhurst did not get his place in Parliament.

The idea was a simple one—that women should be allowed to

vote. In addition, he wanted them to be allowed to serve the community in any way in which they were capable—as councillors, magistrates, mayors and even M.P.s. He did not wish them to be excluded just because they were women.

Three children were born—two daughters and one son. Suddenly Mrs. Pankhurst's happiness was shattered. Her husband died. For most women, the task of bringing up a large family would have been enough. For Emmeline Pankhurst, her husband's death was the beginning. She resolved to carry on his ideas and to win . . . *Votes for Women.*

Like many great movements, the "Women's Social and Political Union" had a very long name and, like most of them, it started in a very small way. In 1903 at 62, Nelson Street, Manchester, a few women met together. They formed their Union under the leadership of Emmeline Pankhurst (supported by her daughters Christabel and Sylvia.) The 'Suffragette' Movement was born. (The word 'suffrage' means the right to vote in Parliamentary elections.) Fortunately the members were all good public speakers and before long they were being asked to address meetings all over the country.

They welcomed these invitations. To win support for their ideas they had to make as many members of the public as possible listen to what they believed. To do this—they had to gain publicity.

Four months later, in February, 1904, a young politician called Winston Churchill was speaking in Manchester. Emmeline Pankhurst tells us that on this occasion she did the most difficult thing in her life—she spoke in front of a vast audience for the first time. She asked Mr. Churchill about his views on Votes for Women. The chairman of the meeting would not accept her question and Mr. Churchill was not called upon to reply. However, her question gained national publicity and was reported in every national newspaper.

The following year gave the W.S.P.U. a bigger opportunity. There had been a General Election (in which only men had been allowed to vote) and the Liberal Party had gained power. To celebrate their victory, a great meeting was held in London's Royal Albert Hall. The new Prime Minister, Sir Henry Campbell-

Bannerman was to speak. Emmeline Pankhurst herself recalls that meeting which would probably have been forgotten quickly had it not been for what she and her friends resolved to do.

Sir Henry, surrounded by his cabinet, made his first utterance as Prime Minister. Previous to the meeting we wrote to Sir Henry and asked him, in the name of the Women's Social and Political Union, whether the Liberal Government would give the vote to women. We added that our representatives would be present at the meeting, and we hoped that the Prime Minister would publicly answer the question. Otherwise we should be obliged publicly to protest against his silence.

Of course Sir Henry Campbell-Bannerman returned no reply, nor did his speech contain any allusion to women's suffrage. So, at the conclusion, Annie Kenney, whom we had smuggled into the hall in disguise, whipped out her little calico banner, and called out in her clear, sweet voice; 'Will the Liberal Government give women the vote?'

At the same moment Theresa Billington let drop from her seat directly above the platform a huge banner with the words: 'Will the Liberal Government give justice to working women?' Just for a moment there was a gasping silence, the people waiting to see what the Cabinet Ministers would do. They did nothing. Then, in the midst of uproar and conflicting shouts, the women were seized and flung out of the hall.

That meeting was important to the Suffragettes. Everybody in the country heard about them. It was important for another reason. Annie Kenney made an important contribution. A tough, intelligent cotton worker in Oldham, she commanded great respect and support among her fellow workers.

With Annie Kenney to help, the activities of Mrs. Pankhurst and her daughters spread. At first the women were not treated badly, but the men in the government were united in their determination to resist the efforts of women to win the vote. Because of this hundreds of other women began to offer their support to the Suffragettes. Rich or poor, young or old, married or single, famous or unknown—they all had one thing in common—a fierce

94

determination to win votes for women.

Money was needed. Both rich and poor members gave generously. At meetings addressed by the Pankhursts or by Annie Kenney, a collection plate was placed by the door and women would put their money into it—as if they were in church.

Before long it was obvious that their peaceful methods were not succeeding. A few Suffragettes were thrown out of public meetings, but on the whole they were ignored and not treated roughly. Indeed, they were often made the subject for jokes. The comedians in the Music Halls sang songs about them—and men in the audience roared with laughter—so did many of the women.

'Put me on an island where the girls are few.
Put me among the most ferocious lions in the zoo.
You can put me on a treadmill, and I'll never, never fret.
But for pity's sake, don't put me near a suffragette.

Even when they went as far as interrupting Members of Parliament while they were actually speaking in the House of Commons, they did not gain much support for their cause—so the Suffragettes made a big decision. They decided to use militant measures. This meant violence—not against people, but against property. They knew they had come to a turning point in their fight. From now on they would be breaking the law. They must expect to be punished by being fined or sent to prison like criminals. For women brought up as they were, this would be terrible ordeal. Holloway Prison (where women prisoners were taken) was bad enough to shock even those who (like Annie Kenney) had not known a life of comfort and leisure.

Young Mary Richardson was only twenty when she joined the Suffragettes. Within a few weeks she had taken part in many meetings and demonstrations. Next she was asked to break windows. Some Suffragettes had attracted a great deal of attention by breaking the large windows of well known shops. Crowds had gathered to watch them being repaired and many photographs were taken and printed in the newspapers.

Mary Richardson was given the job of smashing windows in the Home Office in London's Whitehall. This building was chosen

because it is, from here that the Police Force is controlled by the Home Secretary. His job is to ensure that law and order are maintained throughout the country. To smash these windows would show the country what the Suffragettes thought of the law.

When I arrived in Whitehall it was to find the Home Office guarded by several policemen. I walked past them as casually as I could; but on the corner of Whitehall and Downing Street I turned round quickly and opened fire—one, two, three stones. I had shattered three of the windows before the policemen were able to reach me or even to get their hands free of their cumbersome capes. Those capes must surely have been designed before any idea of quick footed, quick-firing felons like Suffragettes had disturbed the official mind.

Three of us marched off in silence to Cannon Row. It was my first visit to a police station. The intense light inside the place made me blink at first; then I was surprised to find how full of bustle and cheerful conversation it was. It was not until I found myself in a small cell and heard the key turn in the lock of the iron door that I began to shudder.

In the morning a mug of tea was brought in and I made the short journey to Bow Street. Bow Street was as busy a place as the adjacent Covent Garden market. I felt dazed as I was led along a narrow corridor and locked in another, much tinier cell. It had a plank bed with a thin, straw-stuffed pallet and a couple of blankets; and at the end of the bed, as part of it, was an open lavatory. It was a cold, foul place—the foulest place I had ever seen. The rows of cells were arranged like cubicles, open at the top; and there was only one narrow window for all of them, high up in the wall. As I waited I suddenly felt indescribably lonely.

At last the cell door was unlocked and, feeling my limbs quaking under me, I was taken back along the corridor. I stepped into the dock and felt almost comforted by the sight of all the inquisitive faces round me; but, at the same time, I was utterly bewildered. A faint feeling swept over me as I heard the constable tell his story. Words of explanation crowded into my mind; but when the time came for me to speak in my own defence I was struck dumb. I could hardly believe my ears when I heard the magistrate say, 'Six months. Second Division!'

When I was back in my cell I desperately tried to sort out my confused ideas. I was still sorting them out much later when the Black Maria, drawn by two immense horses, rumbled across the cobblestones in the courtyard and I was asked to step inside.

In the swaying, jolting vehicle there was a double row of tiny, coffin-like compartments with a narrow aisle down the centre in which a police officer sat. The compartments were locked. They were so shallow it was impossible to sit properly on the narrow ledge provided. You had to sit sideways and you could not stand up, as the ceiling was too low. All you could do was to shift about in a near crouching position. When one side grew numb you changed to the other.

Mary Richardson did not serve all of her 6-month sentence. Like so many Suffragettes in those early days was allowed home after eleven days. Eleven days without food. The idea of the 'hunger-strike' had proved effective. First the Suffragettes refused

97

all food or drink. Next the prison officers tempted them with delicious dishes. Still they refused. Then they were bullied—but in spite of their weak condition they bravely refused to eat. When it was obvious that the prisoner would die of starvation unless released, the authorities gave way. It was Mary Richardson's first experience of a hunger-strike. She was to know many more—but soon the experience was to be more painful. And ways of keeping the prisoner alive were devised.

In spite of all the meetings and demonstrations—all the damage and all the arrests . . .

. . . and all the sympathy which their imprisonment had aroused, the Suffragettes were still no nearer to winning the vote for women. The government would not give way.

Frustration led some women to desperate measures. By 1913 Queen Victoria's grandson, King George V was on the throne. He was an enthusiastic racegoer—and racehorse owner. In the most famous horserace of all, the Derby run on Epsom Downs, his own horse, Anmer, was strongly fancied to win the race in 1913.

About half way through the $1\frac{1}{2}$ mile race, the horses have to run round a steep bend at a place known as Tattenham Corner.

The English public were growing weary of the activities of the Suffragettes. Race-goers were looking forward to a day on Epsom Downs unspoiled by these ladies and the display of their purple, green and white colours, by their demonstrations and by the appearance of their own newspaper, 'The Suffragette.' They all hoped that it would be the King himself who would lead in the winning horse of the 1913 Derby, his own Anmer.

No special Suffragette activities had been planned by Mrs. Pankhurst and the other leaders. But one woman called Emily Davison was there. So was Mary Richardson—who remembered every moment of that afternoon . . .

That morning, with Ellen's folding stool over one shoulder and my purple, white and green bag with Suffragette literature slung over the other I set off by an early train to Epsom. When I arrived I found the Downs already as busy as a Soho market. People in a noisy, holiday mood were hurrying across the grass, on foot, and crowded inside the old stage coaches and open waggonettes they used then. For some time I sat down on my stool outside the main entrance, having decided not to show my wares until the bigger crowds had arrived. There would be time enough to call attention to myself when people were more settled.

But after people had been going in through the gates for what seemed to me a long time I went on to the course myself and took up a stand near a man who was selling newspapers at one corner of the grandstand. A couple of hours went by. From where I stood it was impossible to see the Royal Box; but I knew by the cheering and the excited faces of the people that Their Majesties had arrived. Just as the first race began I summoned up all my courage and took out a copy of 'The Suffragette' from my bag and waved it in the air. I had judged correctly: except for the scornful glances cast in my direction I was not molested.

It was not until the end of the third race that I saw Emily Davison. We had met several times and from the talks we had had I had formed the opinion that she was a very serious minded person. That was why I felt so surprised to see her. She was not the sort of woman to spend an afternoon at the races. I smiled to her; and from the distance she seemed to be smiling faintly back at me. She stood alone there, close to the white painted rails where the course bends round at Tattenham Corner; she looked absorbed and yet far away from everybody else and seemed to have no interest in what was going on round her. I felt a sudden premonition about her and found my heart was beating excitedly. I shall always remember how calm her face was. But at that very moment—as I was told afterwards by her closest friend—she knew she was about to give her life for the cause.

The evening before the Derby Emily had told a few friends quite calmly that she would be the only casualty. No one else would be injured, not even the jockey.

I was unable to keep my eyes off her as I stood holding 'The Suffragette' up in my clenched hand. A minute before the race started she raised up a paper of her own or some kind of card before her eyes. I was watching her hand. It did not shake. Even when I heard the pounding of the horses' hooves moving closer I saw she was still smiling. And suddenly she slipped under the rail and ran out into the middle of the racecourse. It was all over so quickly. Emily was under the hooves of one of the horses and seemed to be hurled for some distance across the grass. The horse stumbled sideways and its jockey was thrown from its back. She lay very still.

There was an awful silence that seemed to go on for minutes; then, suddenly, angry shouts and cries arose and people swarmed out on to the racecourse. I was rooted to the earth with horror until a man snatched the paper I was still holding in my hand and beat it across my face. That warned me of my own danger. I pushed a way through the crowd and my assailant came pushing his way after me and shouted out to others to stop me. Mercifully I was able to run faster than I had ever run before. I reached the Downs Station not a moment too soon.

Emily Davison was not killed outright—but she died shortly afterwards and her funeral procession brought the Suffragettes together more closely than anything which happened before or after the event. It also won many recruits to the cause. Even the sister of the jockey (who was uninjured) followed behind the hearse bearing Emily Davison's body.

Sometimes the Suffragettes won an unexpected success. On one occasion, Mary Richardson heard that the Bishop of London was to make a speech in the House of Lords against the idea of Votes for Women. She knocked on the door of his London home and asked to see him. He refused. Instead of going away, Mary (standing on the right) and her friend waited.

They waited so long that, at last, the Bishop agreed to see her. He listened to what she had to say. Her arguments were sound. When he made his speech it was to support the Suffragettes—not to oppose them!

With this success to encourage them, the Suffragettes re-doubled their efforts. Having convinced the Bishop of London, Mary Richardson aimed to bring the arguments of her women colleagues to the notice of the King himself. It was learned that George V would be visiting Bristol and travelling through the streets in an open carriage. A petition was signed by thousands of supporters. As it was expected that they might make trouble, all known Suffragettes in Bristol had been warned to keep off the route where the procession would pass. For once they obeyed. All except a visitor to the city . . . Mary Richardson. Clutching her petition (but keeping it out of sight) she joined the crowds in the streets very early in the morning. Much later, the procession came into sight.

The King's carriage, as I had supposed, was surrounded by an escort of cavalry; and beside these came mounted police. I was forced to look sharply and decide quickly behind which horse I would make my dash in order to gain the step of the open carriage. Out I shot then; and, by some miracle, I got to the carriage, leapt on to the step and deposited my petition on the King's knee, keeping my hand on it for a moment as I gasped out, 'A petition, Your Majesty!'

I shall always remember how incredibly blue his eyes were.

The cheering all round me suddenly ceased. There was a moment's deafening silence; then an officer reared up on his horse and struck me with the flat of his sword. (How heavy their swords are!) I spun round. My left shoulder felt as if it had been smashed; I tried to regain my balance, but fell. Instantly a swarm of people seemed to pile on top of me, clawing frenziedly at each other in their efforts to reach me. The police rushed up; but it was some minutes before they were able to extricate me from the struggling mass. By the time they did and when they had stood me on my very shaky legs, I found my clothing had been torn to shreds, my hat gone, my jacket ripped half off, and my skirt was looking more like a kilt. I felt completely dazed and was only too glad to have four strong arms of the law holding on to me and marching me away.

On that occasion she was not imprisoned. The King himself had ordered her release.

She was not always so lucky. She was imprisoned many times. By now, the authorities were not prepared to release a Suffragette just because she went on a hunger strike until she was so weak that they were forced to release her in case she died.

They introduced forcible feeding. This was a barbarous process —designed to keep the women prisoners fed and in reasonably good health against their will. The Suffragettes were shaken when the

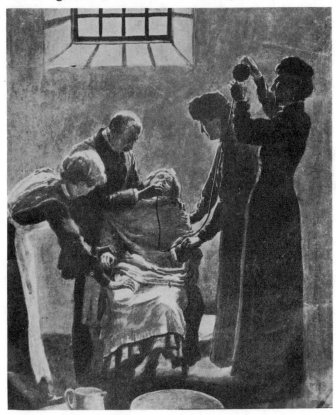

forcible feeding process was started. Those who had endured it were quick to let the public know what it entailed. Posters bearing pictures (p. 103) were issued.

However horrible they looked—and however much they shocked those who saw them, they could not convey the horror of those who endured it. Mary Richardson could never forget the morning when *she* endured it for the first time:

The following morning the horror of forcible feeding was announced by the rumbling of the wheels of the trolley approach-my cell door. I sat down on the floor and pushed my arms under and round the hot-water pipe. I intended to resist to the utmost. As I sat and waited five wardresses came in. They succeeded in loosening my hands to lay me flat on the floor. I struggled with them. By the time I was on my back we were all breathless and panting. To my horror, then, four of the wardresses, who were all hefty women, lay across my legs and body to keep me pinned to the floor. And now that the victim was trussed up and ready the doctors came in dragging the hated trolly at their heels. One knelt to grip my shoulders, another lifted aloft the funnel that was to receive the liquid, the third knelt by my head and took the long tube in his hand . . .

This tube was forced through mouth or nose and a mixture of liquid foods passed through it into the victim's stomach. Like other Suffragettes, Mary Richardson endured this many times. As with many others, it only succeeded in making her more resolute than ever.

What crime could she commit which would be so sensational that it would impress a public already furious about the broken windows, the burnt buildings, the demonstrations, the processions, the petitions?

Concealing a small axe up her sleeve, Mary Richardson made her way to the National Gallery in London's Trafalgar Square. Many of the nation's rarest and most priceless paintings are kept in this building. They are carefully guarded. Mary was an art lover herself—yet she would attempt to destroy one of the most famous and well loved paintings of all . . . The Rokeby Venus by Velasquez.

I went to the Venus room. It looked peculiarly empty. I had to pass in front of the detectives who were sitting on the seat to approach the Velasquez painting. There was a ladder lying against one of the walls, left there by some workmen who had been repairing a sky-light.

As twelve o'clock struck one of the detectives rose from the seat and walked out of the room. The second detective, realizing, I suppose that it was lunch-time and he could relax, sat back, crossed his legs and opened a newspaper.

That presented me with my opportunity—which I was quick to seize. The newspaper held before the man's eyes would hide me for a moment. I dashed up to the painting. My first blow with the axe merely broke the protective glass. But, of course, it did more than that, for the detective rose with his newspaper still in his hand and walked round the red plush seat, staring up at the skylight which was being repaired. The sound of the glass breaking also attracted the attention of the attendant at the door who, in his frantic efforts to reach me, slipped on the highly polished floor and fell face-downwards. And so I was given time to get in a further four blows with my axe before I was, in turn, attacked.

Alone in another 'deafening silence'—that of a cell in Holloway prison—Mary Richardson must have wondered. Had she been right to try and destroy a great work of art—to prevent its being enjoyed by future generations—in the hope that its destruction would make the public change its mind and give votes to women? As it happened, the painting was not seriously damaged and may still be seen in the National Gallery where it is enjoyed by many thousands of visitors each year.

For Mary Richardson there followed more imprisonment, more humiliation—more forcible feeding . . . and eventual release.

In August, 1914, the activities of the Suffragettes were forced off the front pages of the newspapers by news which was much more sensational: WAR with Germany.

The mood and the whole way of life of the nation changed overnight. Men were needed in Europe to fight against the Germans in the First World War. Posters appealed to them from every wall. Britain had to fight, and to win in order to survive. General Kitchener (Commander of our forces) appealed to all men.

Another poster showed the feelings of the women of Britain.

But if the men went—what of the women? Mrs. Pankhurst and her supporters were forced to come to another decision. Should they continue their fight to win the vote for women—or should they pause—and support their country when it needed the help of women as it had never needed it before?

Soon reports and photographs of the battles in Europe reached Great Britain. Hundreds of thousands of our men were killed. Whole cities were destroyed in Europe. Our men suffered indescrible hardships to save our country.

Mrs. Pankhurst summed it up in just one sentence. In answer to the question from some of her supporters—'Why stop the struggle to win votes for women?' she replied:

'What would be the good of a vote—without a country to vote in?'

The campaign of the Suffragettes was halted. Women forgot their grievances. Their country really did need them now.

There would be time enough to fight again when the greater fight was over. Meanwhile, they used their energy to help their country and to support the men who were dying in the trenches of France and all over the world.

Yet, in fact their battle was won. The victory of the Suffragettes was a quiet one. Women proved that they could fight (as Suffragettes) and could work (during the war) in countless jobs where only men had worked before . . .

and they were, at last, given the vote.

A few at first: Women over 30 in 1918. All women over 21 in 1928.

Many Suffragettes did not live to see the victory.

When you see husbands *and* their wives going to vote at your school on Election Days, remember that they do so because of women like Emmeline Pankhurst and Annie Kenney, like Emily Davison and Mary Richardson.

Twentieth Century Cathedral

'D. Day plus 2.' The Allied troops from Britain and many other countries had landed on the French coast two days before.

One great force had been assembled to free Europe from the German armies which had overrun it in 1940. After a terrible journey across the English Channel, the men on shore wondered if the invasion would be successful.

Two young British soldiers among the rest, Basil Spence and Laurie Paynter, wondered would they ever see their families again. Would they survive? Would they be able to start out in a career as people instead of soldiers? Would any of their dreams come true when the long war was over?

Basil Spence remembers this day very well.

On D plus 2, June 1944, I was dug in just off the beaches of Normandy. An army friend, Laurie Paynter, also dug into the ground for protection, asked me just before we fell asleep what my ambition was. The circumstances were such as to set one thinking about such mortal longings. I said, 'To build a Cathedral.'

This remark was, perhaps, prompted by an incident I had witnessed that day. At Oustreham and Hermanville, in the Sword Sector where I had landed, are two beautiful Norman churches. The Germans had placed snipers in each church tower, and in order to winkle them out tanks were brought up which blasted away at the belfry windows. As an architect witnessing the murder of a beautiful building, I felt other ways should have been found to remove those snipers, for I firmly believed that the creative genius of man, the spark of life that he carries while on earth, is lost through the destruction of great works, the world is the poorer, for that particular light has been put out for ever.

Later that year in Brussels I read in an English newspaper that Sir Giles Gilbert Scott, the creator of the magnificent Anglican cathedral at Liverpool had produced a design for the New Coventry Cathedral, and my mind went back to 15th November 1940, when as a Staff Captain (Intelligence) I had reported the Coventry Raid to my General. I remembered telling him that the Cathedral had been destroyed in the night.

The Cathedral at Coventry was not the only one in Britain to be badly damaged during the many air-raids made by German bombers during the Second World War. Exeter suffered as well, but at Coventry, the morning after the raid, when the fires had died down and daylight returned only the walls and the steeple remained standing. It was clear that another Cathedral would have to be built. The original architect's plans for a new building were not satisfactory and in 1947 a unique competition was announced.

The rules were simple—to design a new Cathedral for Coventry. The prize—to see the designs come to life in the new building.

Many architects were very interested in the idea—including Basil Spence who had come through the war.

The competition was all the more exciting because in this century an architect would be able to see his cathedral completed. Many cathedrals had been built in the past and, of course, architects had designed them. But until this time, the actual building had taken so long that the designer had usually died before the building had been finished and he did not have the satisfaction of seeing his cathedral completed.

Nowadays we have so much modern equipment that buildings can be erected much more quickly. The men who built the early cathedrals did not have power driven cranes or lorries or electric saws or mechanical diggers. Today, with the help of these, the work takes less time, uses fewer men and can be just as strong and safe—and beautiful.

The competition was organized by the Bishop and his advisers and they wanted to see what young architects, such as Basil Spence, would suggest for a Cathedral of our own time.

As soon as the competition was announced, Basil Spence decided to visit Coventry to look at the ruins of the old Cathedral and to see if he could decide on any ideas for the design of a new one.

One dull day in October, with no sunshine to brighten the autumn afternoon, my wife and I got into my car and went straight to Coventry. This first visit to the ruined Cathedral was one of the most deeply stirring and moving days I have ever spent.

The bombed Cathedral still had its fine, graceful tower and spire intact, but all that remained of the Cathedral walls was a lace-like screen of masonry, buttresses and pinnacles with perpendicular windows without glass, some with the tracery still there, but others gaping wide.

As soon as I set foot on the ruined nave I felt the impact of delicate enclosure. It was still a cathedral. Instead of the beautiful wooden roof it had the skies as a vault. This was a Holy Place, and although the conditions specified that we need keep only the tower, spire, and the two crypt chapels, I felt I could not destroy this beautiful place, and that whatever else I did, I would preserve as much of the old Cathedral as I could.

The feeling of reverence was intensified as we walked to the stone altar (made from the stones that had fallen inwards after the destruction) and the Charred Cross constructed from roof timbers not quite burnt out, on the altar of the Cross of Nails and behind it the words 'Father Forgive.'

(A few days after the Cathedral had been bombed, the cross made from beams which had fallen from the roof had been tied together with wire and set up at the east end of the old Cathedral. As the roof had burned, large, hand-made nails had fallen down on to the ruined floor. Three of the nails (made 500 years earlier) were put together in the shape of a cross and have become the symbol of Coventry Cathedral. They remind us of the craftsmen who spent most of their lives building the first Cathedral.)

We moved to the North and looked out through the glassless tracery over the ground reserved for the New Cathedral, over St. Michael's Avenue, the gravestones, trees and bombed houses, and in my mind's eye I got one of those pictures that architects sometimes get. This one, however, was unusually clear—a great nave and an altar that was an invitation to Communion, and a huge picture behind it. But, as always with mind pictures, it was ever changing. I could not see the altar clearly but through the bodies of the Saints.

In those few moments the idea of the design was planted. In essence it has never changed.

Although he was very busy with his normal work as an architect, Basil Spence could not put the idea of the new Cathedral at Coventry out of his mind. He knew that many other architects were planning their entries for this great competition. In fact 219 other architects entered their designs by the closing date. He has said that the design was with him day and night. After his day's work was finished, he would work on his plans for the Cathedral until the early hours of the morning. One of his best ideas for the building came in a strange way:

The competition was a testing time for me for several reasons, and as usual in periods of stress and overwork, something went bad—I got an abcess on one of my upper teeth.

My dentist advised immediate extraction with a local anaesthetic. I hate injections and at best I felt queer, but now I was run down and exhausted and I passed out.

My dream was wonderful. I was walking through the Cathedral and it looked marvellous, with a light like Chartres. The altar looked tremendous, backed by a huge tapestry, but I could not see the windows until I went right in and turned half back— the walls were zig—zagged!

He included both these ideas in his final design for the competition. At last the plans were finished and it was time to hand in his entry.

I completed the detail drawing and report and delivered the

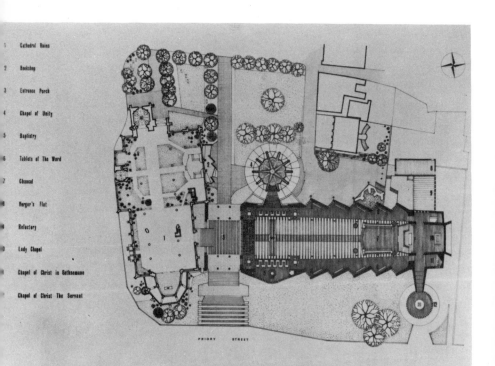

1 Cathedral Ruins

2 Bookshop

3 Entrance Porch

4 Chapel of Unity

5 Baptistry

6 Tablets of The Word

7 Chancel

8 Verger's Flat

9 Refectory

10 Lady Chapel

11 Chapel of Christ in Gethsemane

12 Chapel of Christ The Servant

PRIORY STREET

THE CATHEDRAL CHURCH OF SAINT MICHAEL   COVENTRY

Sir Basil Spence R.A. Architect

drawings personally to Captain Thurston, Secretary of the Reconstruction Committee, on the last day. There were many other architects doing the same thing.

I can say with truth that I did not have the faintest hope of success . . . and right up to the 15th August, 1951, when the results would be announced, I was interested but expected nothing.

On the day of the result, Basil Spence had to go to London for an appointment with a businessman named George Walker. This is how he remembers one of the greatest moments in his life:

In the middle of our discussion the telephone rang. George Walker answered it and said, 'It's for you, they say it's important.'

My secretary's voice said, 'Mr. Spence, good news! Here's Mr. Wearden,' and then Wearden, my Chief Assistant in London, said: 'May I be the first to congratulate you, you've won the competition.'

It is difficult to describe the next few moments, as I cannot remember them very well; swirling mists, a rushing sound in my ears, and I found myself on one of George Walker's comfortable chairs. He was bending over me, his expression all sympathy.

'I'm so terribly sorry, it must be awful news. You look ghastly,' he said.

I stammered, 'It's the best news I've ever had. I have won the Competition for the New Coventry Cathedral.' . . .

It was lunchtime but I felt I had to go to Saint Paul's Cathedral for a while. I went in and stayed under Christopher Wren's great dome quietly for about an hour. I felt a period of dedication was called for as I had a desperate need to be alone and to meditate quietly.

When the excitement of winning the competition was over, Basil Spence had to settle down to a great deal of very hard work indeed. He was disappointed because many people did not like his design. Some of them felt that the modern building which he had designed was not suitable for a Cathedral. Yet he had to have the courage to keep his own ideas unchanged even if important people and other experts suggested that he should change them. Quite frequently their reasons were very good!

Even at this stage more money was needed. Basil Spence had to help to gain as much as possible by touring over Britain and Europe and America to interest people everywhere in helping to rebuild the Cathedral at Coventry.

This was very difficult for him. He was an architect and did not enjoy 'selling' his idea to other people, although he was surprised that so many ordinary men and women who lived miles away from England knew about Coventry and were interested enough to give money to help in the rebuilding.

Before and after the Cathedral was completed, a great deal of valuable help came from one country in particular—from Germany, the country whose planes had dropped the bombs which had destroyed the Cathedral during the war. Probably this gave Basil Spence and all those who wished to see the Cathedral rise again, more pleasure than anything else. Out of the destruction of an old building, grew a great friendship between the people of England in Coventry and the people all over Germany. The Germans helped in many ways—with money, with ideas and with help from parties of young people who came to clear and clean and dig.

At last the site was ready. The new building began to rise from the ground. Countless difficulties were overcome by the architect and his team of experts. All through the building he tried to make his Cathedral as much like his original idea as possible. One part of the building was especially difficult.

The altar, of course, was to be the centre and heart of the building. On his very first visit to Coventry, Basil Spence had visualized a tremendous picture hanging behind the altar. Eventually he decided that a tapestry was the best way of providing a picture with bright, glowing colours which would last for years to come.

An artist was needed who knew *how* to design a tapestry. Weavers were needed to convert the design into the largest tapestry ever made.

It made him very happy when the famous painter, Graham Sutherland agreed to design the tapestry. The painting was superb— but the tapestry was to be 70 feet high by 44 feet across. Where in the world could it be made? Where could the colours in the design be reproduced—and reproduced as that they would not fade over the years?

Finally, a French firm was discovered. Monsieur Pinton (who was in charge of the firm) and Graham Sutherland were able to work out the problems with Basil Spence.

We were breaking all records in tapestry weaving in size and weight, and it must not be forgotten that the method of weaving was the traditional one, and the loom itself was over 500 years old, composed of two great tree-trunks weathered into gentleness by time. How fortunate that this, the longest tapestry loom in the world, *happened* to be the right length with only six inches to spare!

At the same time, Basil Spence was overcoming other problems every day. He planned to have a great statue of St. Michael (the Patron Saint of the Cathedral) outside on a wall near the entrance so that passers by would see it . . . and perhaps be persuaded to enter the Cathedral itself. He decided that the statue must be made by the greatest living sculptor, Sir Jacob Epstein—but he was an old man near the end of his life. However, Epstein agreed.

Yet Epstein was in a hurry. Instead of working slowly away at a 'maquette' (the sculptor's equivalent of a painter's sketch) Sir Jacob was working hard on the final, full-sized statue.

For Basil Spence, this was an exciting but worrying moment. Supposing the Cathedral authorities did not like the finished work? Supposing Epstein's precious time had been wasted. Epstein did not have long to live.

One day I read a newspaper paragraph quoting Sir Jacob as saying that the St. Michael for the new Coventry Cathedral was going to be his greatest work. I rang him up and asked him what was cooking. 'Come and see,' he said.

He was modelling St. Michael in the studio attached to his house, and as I went into the room crowded with plaster casts of great men, beautiful women and children, I had another of the many shocks which attended the building of the Cathedral; not only had Sir Jacob done the maquette but he had started on the full-size figure. The head was done and he had roughed out the torso. It was magnificent, but I was perturbed. 'Sir Jacob,' I said, 'the Committee want to see the 'maquette' and approve it before going on to the full size group.'

'Am I going too fast?' he asked; then after a moment added, 'Look, I'm not working for the Committee any more, I am working for myself.'

I telephoned the Provost and the Bishop and they came next day to see Sir Jacob and St. Michael. Without a moment's hesitation they both praised it. They said they wanted to see nothing else as the head was truly wonderful. Photographs were taken that day, an emergency meeting of the Cathedral Council and the Reconstruction Committee was called in Coventry and

Sir Jacob's work was approved.

This was his last great work before he died.

New ideas were being built into the Cathedral so that it became a true place of worship for the Twentieth Century. There was a chapel (called the Chapel of Unity) where people of all denominations can worship. There was a special room for men and women working in the many factories around Coventry. Some visitors think that the 'Gethsemane Chapel' built for private prayer is the most beautiful part of the Cathedral.

Meanwhile, the ruins of the old Cathedral were being tidied and repaired so that they would be able to stand up to any weather conditions. They were linked in a very clever way to the new Cathedral. When visitors leave the old ruins, they walk down a flight of steps and can see right into the new building through a great wall of glass. On this are engraved pictures of the Saints—just as Basil Spence had imagined when he first visited Coventry. At the end of the long nave, past the graceful pillars, the glowing colours of Graham Sutherland's magnificent tapestry can be seen.

Thousands of people were at Coventry when the opening Service of Consecration was held in May, 1962. The Queen herself was present and since that day, millions of people from Britain and from the rest of the world have visited Coventry to see this Twentieth Century Cathedral.

It was a proud day for Basil Spence—but his thoughts must have gone back to a much smaller ceremony when the tiny 'Chapel of the Cross' was ready for worship in the new building long before the whole Cathedral was finished.

At that time, the priest in charge of the Cathedral was Provost Howard—but with the completion of the new building in sight, he felt it was time for him to retire and hand over to a younger man.

During the service, when the altar was being blessed, the old Provost carried the naked flame from the altar in the crypt chapel in the old Cathedral. With great dignity he handed the torch to the new Provost, who slowly lit the candles on the new altar. As their light flickered into being we all knew that spiritual

life had been transferred at last from the old Cathedral to the new.

Once the final ceremony of consecration had taken place, the newspapers of England, Britain, Europe—and the World were quick to respond to the importance of the event.

Countless photographs were taken, special booklets were issued—and the help of many nations was acknowledged. The gratitude of all connected with the re-building was reported in full.

Coventry Cathedral—its worship, its praise, its thanksgiving and its hopes for the future were there for all to see and to read.

List for Further Study

Throughout this book, the words of the person who was actually present at an important event in the Twentieth Century, have been used when ever possible.

If you are interested in finding out more about any of the events described, the following books will help you. There are many more. Your school and Public Library will be glad to help you in your search for more information. Quotations in the text were taken from the books marked with an asterisk.

SCOTT OF THE ANTARCTIC
Scott's Last Expedition (John Murray)*
The Voyage of the 'Discovery' (John Murray)
The Voyages of Captain Scott, J. M. Barrie, (Smith, Elder & Co.)
Captain Scott, L. Du Garde Peach, (A Ladybird Book—Wills & Hepworth)
Scott of the Antarctic, Reginald Pound (Cassell)
Heroes of Polar Exploration, Ralph K. Andrist (Cassell)

Pictures may be obtained from the National Portrait Gallery, a visit to the *Discovery* in London is worthwhile and listening to 'Sinfonia Antarctica' by Sir Ralph Vaughan Williams gives a picture in sound of the bleak wastes of Antarctica.

'TITANIC'
A Night to Remember, Walter Lord (Rinehart & Winston)

THE WOODEN HORSE
The Wooden Horse, Eric Williams (Collins)*

KON-TIKI
The Kon-Tiki Expedition, Thor Heyerdahl (George Allen & Unwin)*

FOUR MINUTE MILE
First Four Minutes, Roger Bannister (Putnam)*

20TH CENTURY CATHEDRAL
Phoenix at Coventry, Basil Spence (Geoffrey Bles Ltd)*
A visit to the Cathedral itself is essential to understand the conception of a Cathedral for the 20th. Century. There is a variety of beautifully produced booklets, photographs and colour transparencies available from the Cathedral Bookshop in Coventry.

CLIMBING MOUNT EVEREST
The Ascent of Everest, Sir John Hunt (Hodder & Stoughton)*
Sir John Hunt's picture edition of this book is valuable for those studying the subject.

ANNE'S DIARY
The Diary of Anne Frank, Anne Frank (Vallentine Mitchell & Co.)*
This book is also available as a Paperback published by Pan Books.

THE MAN WHO WALKED IN SPACE
The U.S. Information Service is glad to supply material (booklets, photographs, etc.) relating to American Space Exploration. The quotations used were taken from:
A Walk in Space—Gemini 4—Extravehicular Activity (U.S. National Aeronautics & Space Administration)*

VOTES FOR WOMEN
Laugh A Defiance, Mary Richardson (George Weidenfield & Nicolson)*
My Story, Christabel Pankhurst
The True Book About Emmeline Pankhurst, Harold Campion (Muller)*
The Emancipation of Women, M. N. Duffy (Basil Blackwell)
A useful book for discovering eyewitness accounts of those and other events in the 20th. Century is:
They Saw It Happen Vol IV., Asa Briggs (Basil Blackwell)

All these events were seen or are remembered by men and women still alive today. Usually they are glad to talk about their memories to younger people. Public Libraries and newspapers have files of old newspapers and magazines. If you are careful with these valuable documents, they will be glad to show them to you. Shops selling second-hand goods often have piles of old books and magazines for sale at a low price. Searching for them in these places—and in attics and cellars is an exciting and rewarding occupation. You will be surprised what you can uncover in these places.